Mander Portman Woodward (
the UK's best-known groups o
sixth-form colleges. We have mo
experience of guiding student
application procedures for higher education and
helping them to achive the high grades they
need. We cover a wide range of A-level and
GCSE subjects in courses lasting from 10 weeks
(the shortests retakes) to two years. We teach in
small groups or individually. MPW offers a
unique blend of expert tuition, close
supervision, study skills and exam technique. It
is a combination which generates impressive
exam results and gives our students the
confidence and qualifications they need to win a
place in higher education.

MPW Guides have been written in order to
provide our students with the best possible
advice on higher education. They cover the
entrance procedures for Medicine, Dentistry,
Veterinary Science, Law, Psychology, Business &
Management and The Media. On a more general
level, there is a guide to help applicants
complete their UCAS forms and advice on
entrance to Oxford and Cambridge, the Clearing
System and a survival manual for the sixth-form.
We are grateful to Trotman and Company for
helping us to make the Guides available to a
wider audience.

*If you would like to know more about MPW or MPW
Guides, please telephone us on 020 7584 8555.*

The Trotman Web Site

The Trotman Publishing Web Site has been developed for all those interested in careers and higher education.

Each address has its own distinct function, and all are accessible from the Trotman Publishing home page (www.trotmanpublishing.co.uk). Bookmark these sites and benefit from using our online services.

www.trotmanpublishing.co.uk
All our company information at the click of a mouse button

- Publication dates – know what is coming and when
- Read reviews of books – what other people have said about them
- *Win Your Rent* online entry
- Contact us – give us your feedback
- Special offers – take advantage of seasonal offers

www.careers-portal.co.uk
A links portal site dedicated to careers guidance

- 1,700 links in an easy-to-use search format
- Use the search facility to locate sites by subject
- Voted by The Daily Mail one of the Top Ten careers sites

www.careersuk.co.uk
The UK's only online e-commerce bookstore dedicated to careers

- Over 300 careers-related book and CD-ROM titles
- Fast database interrogation allows searches by title, author, subject or ISBN
- Order directly over the internet using our secure credit card facility

So whatever you want to know about careers resources, news or organisations, it's available online from
Trotman

How to Complete Your

UCAS

Form

for 2001 entry

TONY HIGGINS

BA, HonDEd, FIMgt, FRSA

Chief Executive
Universities and Colleges Admissions Service

TROTMAN

This twelfth edition published in 2000
by Trotman and Company Limited,
2 The Green, Richmond, Surrey TW9 1PL

© Trotman and Company Limited 2000

British Library Cataloguing in Publication Data

A catalogue record for this book is available from the British Library

ISBN 0-85660-534-4

Typeset by Type Study, Scarborough, North Yorkshire

Printed and bound in Great Britain by Creative Print & Design (Wales) Ltd

Exploit your maths skills and
YOU'LL NEVER LOOK BACK

A nationally recognised centre of excellence, we provide an extensive range of facilities and courses strongly linked to business and industry. Our innovative approach offers effective and up-to-the minute training for the professions giving us one of the best graduate employment records in the UK.

Statistics/Management Science

If you have a Mathematics or Statistics qualification beyond GCSE, we'll develop your computing and quantitative skills and your understanding of professional business - making you immediately valuable to a wide range of top employers.

Our highly specialised but practical degree programmes offer successful career routes into business analysis and development, statistical analysis, management services and operational research

- BSc(Honours) Applied Statistics
- BSc(Honours) Management Science

Computing

A crucial area of professional expertise for the future, computing offers unsurpassed employment prospects to suitably qualified graduates.

For students with mathematical flair we can make the most of your talents in our exciting new degree course

- BSc(Honours) Computing (Visualisation)

Or, you can combine both subject areas in

- BSc(Honours) Computing and Management Sciences

We also offer a range of specialist computing courses closely related to the professional world of IT

- BSc(Honours) Business Information Systems
- BSc(Honours) Computing (Networks and Communication)
- BSc(Honours) Computing (Software Engineering)
- BSc(Honours) European Computing
- HND Computing Programme

For further information please telephone 0114 225 2131

Or contact School of Computing and Management Sciences
Sheffield Hallam University City Campus Howard Street Sheffield S1 1WB
E-mail ugcms@shu.ac.uk www.shu.ac.uk/

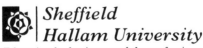

Sheffield
Hallam University
Education for business and the professions

Sh✺✺t straight into a j✺b

Riding High
In the last ten years, Manchester's UMIST university has won 3 Queen's Prizes for Higher Education, 2 Prince of Wales' Awards for Innovation and 2 Queen's Awards for Export.

£££ Reward
A Sunday Times survey, in February 2000, showed that UMIST graduates earn the highest salaries in Britain. Six months after graduation, the top earner was being paid £63,000 whilst the median salary was £18,300).

Hot Shot Careers
97.8% of UMIST graduates were either in work or continuing their studies 6 months after graduation (1999 HESA survey). Employers have regularly voted the joint UMIST/Manchester Careers Service the top in the UK. Many of our degree courses include a year with employers.

Quick on the Draw
Join us now. Contact us on Tel: 0161 200 4033   or Fax: 0161 200 8765   email: ug.admissions@umist.ac.uk or check us out on the web: www.umist.ac.uk

UMIST **Your Better Future**

Contents

Author's Note

The process of getting a place at university or college has two stages: **research** and **self-presentation**. The purpose of research is to make an informed choice of courses and institutions, taking account of your own ambitions, interests and strengths. Then you need to present yourself effectively. There are so many applicants that many decisions have to be taken without interview. The UCAS application form therefore becomes the most important way for you to influence the admissions tutor's decision. By definition your application form will be the *first* contact you have with the admissions tutor. Indeed it may be the *only* contact you have. This guide is intended to help *you* complete *your* form in the most effective way.

Here and there are particular items of advice that

you may find *particularly useful*. These are marked

Examples of what *not* to do are marked

My thanks are due to UCAS for permission to copy the application form.

The 2001 entry edition of the *UCAS Directory* is not available when this book is prepared, and there may be minor changes affecting (for example) the models given for section 3. Please ensure that you check items such as this in the new *Directory*.

The views expressed in this book are my own, not necessarily those of UCAS.

I am particularly grateful to my colleague, Stephen Lamley of Lancaster University without whose work this book would not have been possible and also to my Personal Assistant, Lynn Allen whose help with the manuscript has been invaluable.

This book is intended to help applicants complete the paper UCAS application form. Increasing numbers of students are applying electronically direct into the UCAS computer. The principles underlying the completion of the paper-based form are, however, equally valid for the electronic version. The development of electronic systems at UCAS is proceeding so quickly that we can expect the majority of applications to be filed electronically in perhaps two years' time.

While the principles behind the ideas contained in this book are appropriate for all applicants to higher education, much of it is written for the majority of applicants ie 18-year-old school and college leavers. When they sign the UCAS application form it could well be the first formal, life-deciding document they have signed in their own right. For example, it has previously nearly always been a parental decision as to where they were educated or where they lived. Now it is the young person's turn! It is his or her life, future, choice, decision and responsibility. Parents should help and guide but not force! To this end Trotman, in association with UCAS, publishes a guide for parents entitled *The Complete Parents' Guide to Higher Education* available from Trotman.

Tony Higgins
February 2000

USE BLACK BALLPOINT OR BLACK TYPE AND BLOCK CAPITALS ON PAGE 1

APPLICATION FORM FOR ENTRY IN **2001**

Attach your application fee and completed acknowledgement card here with a paperclip ⬆

YOU MUST READ *HOW TO APPLY* BEFORE COMPLETING THE FORM IN BLACK INK

 Awarded for excellence

UCAS

Return completed form to:
Universities and Colleges Admissions Service
PO Box 67, Cheltenham, Glos GL52 3ZD

111
SAMPLE

1 TITLE/NAME/ADDRESS   Title

Surname/Family name

First/given name(s)

Postal Address line 1

Address line 2

Address line 3

Address line 4

Postcode (UK only)

These boxes for UCAS use only
APR
COB
NAT
LEA

| A | AS | H | C | W | P |
| VOC | HSC | ILC | M | WR | OEG |

Main contact number (including STD/area code)   Tel: Fax:

Home contact number (including STD/area code)   Tel: Fax:

email

email

2 FURTHER DETAILS

Your age on 30 September 2001: Years   Months

Male (M)/Female (F)

Date of birth

Disability/special needs (including dyslexia)/medical condition

Date of first entry to live in the UK

Residential category

Area of permanent residence

Country of birth

Nationality

Student Registration Number for vocational qualifications or Scottish Candidate Number (SCN)

Student Support Arrangements

Fee code

Previous Surname/Family name

Home address (if different)

Postcode (UK only)

3 APPLICATIONS IN *UCAS DIRECTORY* ORDER

If you wish to apply later for Art & Design Route B courses please tick (✓)

(a) Institution code name	(b) Institution code	(c) Course code	(d) Campus code	(e) Short form of the course title	(f) Further details requested in the *UCAS Directory*	(g) Point of entry	(h) Home	(j) Defer entry

If you have previously applied to any institution(s) listed above enter the institution code(s) and your most recent UCAS application number (if known)

4 SECONDARY EDUCATION/FE/HE

	From Month	Year	To Month	Year	PT, FT or SW	UCAS SCHOOL OR COLLEGE CODE

5 Tick (✓) if you have a National Record of Achievement or Progress File (UK applicants only)   pre-16 ☐   post-16 ☐

6 ADDITIONAL INFORMATION (not used for selection purposes)

A   Occupational Background_____

B   Ethnic Origin (UK applicants only)

C   UCAS may send you information from other organisations about products and services directly relevant to higher education applicants. Please tick the box if you do *not* want to receive it. ☐

Page 1

X

7A QUALIFICATIONS COMPLETED (Examinations or assessments (including key/core skills) for which results are known, including those failed)

Examination/Assessment centre number(s) and name(s)

Examination(s)/Award(s)						Result Grade	Examination(s)/Award(s)						Result Grade
Month	Year	Awarding body	Subject/unit/module/ component		Level/ qual	Mark or Band	Month	Year	Awarding body	Subject/unit/module/ component		Level/ qual	Mark or Band

7B QUALIFICATIONS NOT YET COMPLETED (Examinations or assessments (including key/core skills) to be completed, or results not yet published)

Examination/Assessment centre number(s), name(s) and address(es)

Examination(s)/Award(s)						Result	Examination(s)/Award(s)						Result
Month	Year	Awarding body	Subject/unit/module/ component		Level/ qual		Month	Year	Awarding body	Subject/unit/module/ component		Level/ qual	

xi

8 SPECIAL NEEDS or SUPPORT required as a consequence of any disability or medical condition stated in Section 2.						

9 DETAILS OF PAID EMPLOYMENT TO DATE Names and addresses of recent employers	Nature of work	From		To		PT/ FT
		Month	Year	Month	Year	

10 PERSONAL STATEMENT (do NOT attach additional pages or stick on additional sheets)

Name of applicant

11 CRIMINAL CONVICTIONS: Do you have any criminal convictions? See *How to Apply* YES ☐ NO ☐

12 DECLARATION: I confirm that the information given on this form is true, complete and accurate and no information requested or other material information has been omitted. I have read *How to Apply*, I undertake to be bound by the terms set out in it and I give my consent to the processing of my data by UCAS and educational institutions. I accept that, if I do not fully comply with these requirements, UCAS shall have the right to cancel my application and I shall have no claim against UCAS or any higher education institution or college in relation thereto.

	tick one
I have attached payment to the value of £15.00/£5.00	
or	
I have attached a completed credit/debit card payment coupon	

Applicant's Signature.. Date ....

REMEMBER TO KEEP A PHOTOCOPY – SEE APPLICANT CHECKLIST ON BACK OF *HOW TO APPLY*

Page 3

xii

REFERENCE

Do **NOT** attach additional pages

UCAS

PO Box 67, Cheltenham, Glos GL52 3ZD
UCAS is a Registered Educational Charity
UCAS Ref No UC-0003A/01

444

SAMPLE

Name of referee	Type of school, college or training centre	
Post/Occupation/Relationship	Dates when the applicant is unavailable for interview due to examinations, etc.	
Name and address of school/college/organisation		
	Total number in post-16 education	Full time
		Part time
Tel: Fax:	Number normally proceeding to higher education each year	
email:		

Name of applicant (block capitals or type)

Section 7 checked as correct?	Yes	
Correct fee and stamped acknowledgement card enclosed?	Yes	

Referee's Signature: _____

Date: _____

SEE REFEREE CHECKLIST ON BACK OF *HOW TO APPLY*

APPLICATIONS FLOWCHART

*Standard UCAS Applications and
Route A (simultaneous) Art & Design Applications*

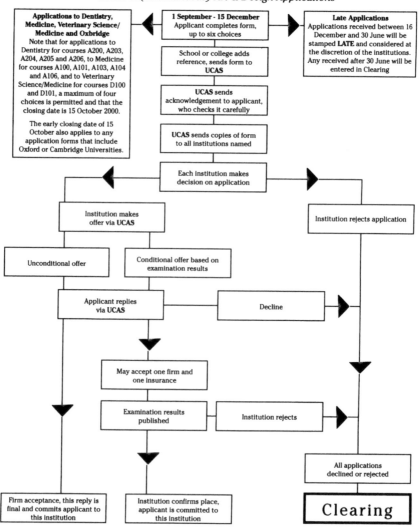

Applications to Dentistry, Medicine, Veterinary Science/ Medicine and Oxbridge
Note that for applications to Dentistry for courses A200, A203, A204, A205 and A206, to Medicine for courses A100, A101, A103, A104 and A106, and to Veterinary Science/Medicine for courses D100 and D101, a maximum of four choices is permitted and that the closing date is 15 October 2000.

The early closing date of 15 October also applies to any application forms that include Oxford or Cambridge Universities.

1 September - 15 December
Applicant completes form, up to six choices

School or college adds reference, sends form to **UCAS**

UCAS sends acknowledgement to applicant, who checks it carefully

UCAS sends copies of form to all institutions named

Late Applications
Applications received between 16 December and 30 June will be stamped **LATE** and considered at the discretion of the institutions. Any received after 30 June will be entered in Clearing

Each institution makes decision on application

Institution makes offer via **UCAS**

Institution rejects application

Unconditional offer

Conditional offer based on examination results

Applicant replies via **UCAS**

Decline

May accept one firm and one insurance

Examination results published

Institution rejects

All applications declined or rejected

Firm acceptance, this reply is final and commits applicant to this institution

Institution confirms place, applicant is committed to this institution

Clearing

xiv

Introduction

If you want to go to university or college for a full-time course at degree, HND or undergraduate diploma level, you will have to fill in a UCAS application form. Most applicants will wish to apply for more than one course, up to the maximum number of choices permitted by the UCAS form (ie six): for this there is an application fee of £15. If you wish to apply to a single course you may do so at a charge of £5.

However, if later you wish to add an additional choice or choices you will be charged an additional £10 ie the difference between the single and multiple choice fee.

There is also a facility for a two-phase application process for those who wish to apply for courses in Art and/or Design.

This book aims to help you complete the application form to the best advantage. Making a good job of your form is one of the essentials if you are to get a place in a popular subject. But in any subject, if you present yourself well you will give yourself the best chance of getting offers of places, and thus finding the university or college which is best for you.

This book also contains advice on applying realistically. It does not guarantee acceptance, and inevitably it contains generalisations. Before you pick up a UCAS form or sit in front of the computer it is important to do your own research. Try to understand yourself, your abilities and your aptitudes. Going to university or college is a crucial point in your life, and it deserves to have time spent on it!

The form itself may be the first important application form you have had to complete. Some basic points are:

- Photocopy a blank form and do a draft before attempting the real thing.
- Use black ink so that when UCAS has copied it and reduced it to about half size it will still be legible.
- Write very clearly – if admissions tutors cannot decipher your writing, you are wasting your time and theirs.
- When you have finished it, keep a photocopy (or your draft) so that you can remind yourself what you said before any interviews.
- Above all, present yourself in the most effective way you can – think: *what impression am I going to create?*

WHAT IS UCAS?

UCAS stands for the Universities and Colleges Admissions Service. Its functions are to organise and regulate the process of entry to full-time and sandwich first degree, DipHE and HND courses in all the UK universities (except the Open University) and most other colleges.

UCAS does *not* take decisions on applications. All these decisions are taken by the institutions you name on your form. It is they who will decide whether or not to offer you a place.

The UCAS computer then records all decisions made about you, and generates the official notifications that are sent to you. You may receive a letter direct from a university or college but it is the UCAS letter that contains the official decision. Nowadays nearly every institution has a computer link to the UCAS offices in Cheltenham, enabling it to transmit offers and rejections, to receive

2

information about your replies, and to produce its own statistics.

The institutions named on your form will see the other institutions to which you have applied. All the universities and colleges to which you have applied will have access to your full UCAS computer record (except your answers to section 6 of the application form – see pages 69–70), so that each of them will know what decisions the other listed universities and colleges have taken.

Preparing to Apply

LEAVE PLENTY OF TIME

Decide in good time whether you want to go into higher education or not. This is a stage in your life where nothing is automatic. Make a conscious decision whether you want to go on with your education. Do you really want to spend several more years in a learning environment? If so, why? Because of job prospects? Because you have a real academic or vocational interest you want to pursue? Because you will *enjoy* it?

Ask yourself these questions, and be honest with yourself. You need to feel *committed, motivated*; otherwise you will not do well, and may even drop out or fail. It is important that you choose courses and institutions that you will *enjoy*. When was the last time you were really successful at something you did not enjoy?

If you are not sure, think about a 'year out' to help you decide, free of pressure at school or college. With some 33 per cent of 18-year-olds going into higher education each year, turning down a place, or not applying, needs careful thought too.

RESEARCH POSSIBLE CAREERS

If you have a particular career in mind, find out about it. First-hand experience, through work experience or work shadowing, is particularly valuable when you are thinking of committing yourself to a lifelong career.

At the very least you need to know:

• What is it like to do this job? (Talk to people, find out how they spend their time.)

5

- What kind of degree or diploma do you need? (It may not even be a degree in a particular subject – as in Accountancy: but it may be a degree of a particular standard – as in Law.)
- What further training will you have to undertake after your degree? (How long? Where? Is it paid? How many employers take on trainees?)
- How might this job prepare you for an alternative career in due course? People are increasingly switching careers at least once during their lives.

RESEARCH POSSIBLE COURSES

Choose possible courses.

There is no substitute here for sheer hard work but there are certain computerised guidance tools which can give considerable help, among them *Centigrade*, *Discourse* and *Coursefinder*. UCAS supports *Centigrade* – a psychometric test/interest questionnaire which assesses both your academic and personal strengths and weaknesses and then suggests what subject areas or courses it might be worth your while researching in some detail. About a quarter of all schools and colleges already use this system but if yours does not you could contact the suppliers of *Centigrade* direct for your own individual test. They are Cambridge Occupational Analysts Ltd, The Old Rectory, Sparham, Norwich NR9 5AQ. The cost is £12.50 per person and you are advised to do it with the help of a teacher at school or college. Costs are cheaper if a school or college puts a number of students through the test.

- Check that you have the necessary GCSEs, and are taking suitable A or AS-levels, Scottish Highers or Advanced Highers, BTEC, Advanced GNVQ (shortly to be renamed Vocational A-levels) or other qualifications.
- Find out about the course content. Even if it is a

school subject, it may be very different at university or college level: for example, English will often include historical or modern English language as well as English literature, and literature may well include critical theory and other aspects of the subject that are new to you.

- Do some research. Three or four years is a long time to devote to a subject – so find out what it includes, and how it is taught and assessed. Don't choose a subject simply because 'it sounds interesting' – that should be just the starting point.
- If you are interested in combined or modular courses, which can often provide very interesting interdisciplinary approaches (eg in European Studies or Communication Studies or Combined Science), be aware that you may have to make your own connections between the components, and that the work in the different subjects may not be well coordinated (that's why students say that combined or joint degrees, even in only two subjects, are hard work!). Or are you choosing a combined course as a means of not making up your mind? Would a 'major' and 'minor' be better for you than an equal combination of two subjects?

TIP
- If you are not absolutely sure about your choice, look for institutions where it is possible to switch courses during or after the first year.

REFERENCE SOURCES

Use reference sources sensibly. The most important are:

- The UCAS World Wide Web Site (http://www.ucas.com) provides a course search facility by qualification (eg degree or HND), subject, geographical area and university or college. This links into all university and college websites which usually carry information on course content, examination arrangements and entry qualifications. It is linked to the *Student UK* website – the most up-to-date site on student affairs.

- The *UCAS Directory* (available to all schools and colleges, public libraries, citizens advice bureaux and careers services) and £6 to UK addresses from UCAS, PO Box 67, Cheltenham, Glos. GL52 3ZD, or telephone 01242 223707 or fax 01242 544960 or email: app.req@ucas.ac.uk
- *University and College Entrance: The Official Guide* (also known as *The Big Book*) published by UCAS and available from Sheed & Ward Ltd, 14 Coopers Row, London EC3 2BH.
- *Entrance Guide to Higher Education in Scotland* published by UCAS in association with the Committee of Scottish Higher Education Principals.
- *Studylink UK* is the official multimedia CD-ROM published by UCAS on behalf of the higher education sector. It is both a sound and video version of prospectuses as well as an essential electronic source of information on entry to higher education courses.
- *Go Higher* is a three-part video made by UCAS with the BBC (starring Mark Radcliffe and 'Lard') and sets out all you need to know about how to get into higher education and stay there! Available from UCAS.
- *Sponsorship for Students* published by CRAC, 159–173 St John Street, London EC1V 4DR.
- *The Potter Guide to Higher Education* published by Dalebank Books, 4 Old Grammar School, School Gardens, Shrewsbury SY1 2AJ.
- *Degree Course Offers* by Brian Heap, published by Trotman & Co Ltd.
- *What University or College* sponsored by BBC Radio 1 and published jointly by On Course Publications and UCAS.

Trotman also publishes a wide range of other useful books, including *Getting into Oxford* and *Cambridge, Students' Money Matters, Clearing the Way.* The 'Getting into' series gives information on degree course and career subjects such as *Medicine, Veterinary Science, Media, Sport & Leisure, Music, Drama & Dance, Journalism, Paramedical Sciences, Tourism, Financial Services, Teaching,* and many more. For detailed course listings in subjects of specific interest to you, check in the new UCAS-Trotman Complete Guides 2001 series: *Art & Design, Engineering, Business, Physical Sciences, Medical & Allied Professions, Performing Arts,* and *Computer Sciences.*

MAKE A SHORT LIST

Make a fairly short list (say, up to 12) of institutions you think may be suitable for you (and whose grade requirements you think you might meet), and write to them for prospectuses.

You *must* read carefully the prospectuses of any course you are really interested in (and keep the prospectuses of those to which you apply). You will be able to connect directly with the websites of the institutions you are interested in from the UCAS website. However, it is advisable to make a short list of possible universities and colleges before assembling your own collection. Remember that prospectuses are written to impress you, and keep in mind questions such as:

- What will I actually spend my time studying?
- What range of choice will I have?
- What does it say about tutorial arrangements and advice?
- How will my work be assessed?
- Where will I live?
- What kind of environment will it be?

- What qualifications do I need in order to get a place?

This last point is very important. If you still have to take your school or college leaving examinations you will need to be very clear about the grades you think you will achieve. It would be a waste of an application if you chose an institution which normally asks for grades higher than those you are likely to get. *University and College Entrance: The Official Guide* and *Degree Course Offers* can help here.

If you are thinking of applying to a course for which competition for places is very severe, eg Medicine, it may be worth checking with the Department(s) concerned to find out if there are any 'hidden' requirements, eg specific subjects and/or grades at GCSE or appropriate work experience.

TIP

Universities and colleges are beginning to develop Entry Profiles which are available on their websites. These profiles detail all the academic and non-academic criteria against which students are selected. It is worth searching the UCAS website for these although they are only in their early stage of development.

TIP

With an eye to the future, go through the prospectuses with a pencil or highlighter, picking out the things that impress you, and those on which you will want more information. This will help you if you go for interview (which may be months later) and are asked why you chose that institution and that course.

GNVQ STUDENTS

The Advanced GNVQ (AGNVQ) is a relatively new qualification and some are unsure of how it prepares students for entry to higher education in

10

comparison with the more conventional A-levels. As from the school/college year beginning in September 2000 the Advanced GNVQ is to be renamed The Vocational A-level. This should help with its understanding.

Much of the advice routinely given to potential applicants is also directly relevant to GNVQ applicants. The need to research choices carefully prior to application is of fundamental importance. This involves careful consideration of the institution (type, environment, accommodation available and recreational facilities) and course (content, structure, entry requirements, nature of teaching and assessment, career options).

Although Advanced GNVQs are benchmark entry requirements for most higher education institutions (HEIs), the level of awareness inside many HEIs is mixed. A lack of understanding about any educational qualification can lead to a frustrating lack of information for those applicants about the acceptability of their qualifications for entry to a course, and a reluctance on behalf of some individual admissions tutors to recruit students from 'unfamiliar' routes.

Because GNVQs are still relatively new and developing qualifications, it is essential that GNVQ applicants research the alternatives available to them thoroughly, both in terms of course and institution.

Issues frequently raised by HEIs in relation to the entry of applicants with GNVQs to higher education courses include the following:

Recognition of key skills
- Advanced GNVQ programmes require students to have achieved level 3 in the key skills of

Application of Number, Communication and Information Technology. A well-focused investigation is occurring into how the key skills of Application of Number and Communication equate with the more subject-based GCSEs in Mathematics and English. It is generally recognised that key skills do enhance a student's understanding of the subject content of the GCSEs by encouraging the application of aspects of Mathematics and English to a vocational context.

However, there are some issues relating to the depth of coverage of certain mathematical concepts (for example: calculus) and aspects of English (for example: essay-writing) that are important for successful progression to particular higher education courses.

Therefore, where a higher education course has entry requirements of GCSE grade Cs in English and Mathematics, applicants should not apply to those HEIs without the appropriate GCSEs.

Entry criteria

- Some HEI admissions tutors are selecting for very popular courses and as a result ask for very high grades from GCE A-level applicants. Where this is the case, but the HEI admissions tutor has agreed to accept GNVQ students, it is very likely that the Advanced GNVQ applicant will be required to get a distinction, possibly also with additional studies. If this is the case, and an applicant is not predicted to achieve a distinction grade, then the applicant should not choose that course at that particular HEI.

Subject knowledge at entry

- For some degree courses, HEIs stipulate an entry requirement which includes a named GCE A-level, to a **high** grade. Although this may be a method of restricting entry to popular courses, for some degree courses it is necessary to have a depth of conceptual understanding at entry to the course. Where this is acquired through subject knowledge, and is a prerequisite for degree success, it is unlikely that these courses will be available to Advanced GNVQ students, **unless** they have completed the required GCE A-level alongside their Advanced GNVQ.

Styles of assessment

- Although HEIs are increasingly moving their own courses and structures towards a broader range of assessment styles, there are some institutions where assessment is still based on essay-writing techniques in a series of unseen examinations. Other HEIs have moved towards open-book examinations and continuous assessment.

TIP

It may be more appropriate for GNVQ applicants who are less confident with unseen examinations, to focus on courses and institutions where there is a greater emphasis on the continuous assessment approach with which they are familiar as a result of success during their GNVQ programme.

Geographical range of HEIs

- Many applicants apply to a broad range of courses but at only one HEI. Unless choice is necessarily restricted in this way, perhaps for personal reasons, it is unwise to apply to one institution only. Unless that institution as a whole and the admissions tutors in particular are positive about AGNVQs, most or all choices are wasted at the outset, irrespective of other issues such as entry requirements or key skills. Also, it can be difficult (although not impossible) to justify a broad range of courses especially where these cross a number of vocational/academic subject areas.

Relevance of cultural studies

- Although GNVQs have been designed to provide general education within a vocational context, evidence from current Advanced GNVQ applicants indicates that their choice of degree courses closely reflects the subject areas of their Advanced GNVQ programmes. Until the general education content of GNVQs is better understood by applicants and admissions tutors, it is important for applicants to pay particular attention to justifying their choice of HE courses and the linkage with their present learning programmes, especially where the linkage is not evident from the GNVQ titles.

TIP

Many HEIs are very positive about GNVQ applicants. It is essential that applicants refer to prospectuses and *University and College Entrance* to research HEI choice effectively.

YOUR TIMETABLE

- If you are on a two-year sixth-form or college course, all the preparatory work needs to be done by *September* – more than a year before you will start in higher education. If you are on a one-year course, you are still working to the same application deadlines, but do not neglect your preparation.

Application deadline

- If you apply by 15 December all universities and colleges guarantee to consider your application. Applying after that date is to be avoided unless you are applying through Route B for Art and Design (see pages 22 and 27). If you wish to apply for a degree course leading to a professional qualification in medicine, dentistry or veterinary science or to Oxford or Cambridge University then 15 October is the deadline. This is also the deadline for the additional Cambridge Preliminary Application Form (PAF) or the Oxford application card. No other universities or

14

colleges in the UCAS system have their own application forms but a handful of universities, as indicated in the *UCAS Directory*, ask for a direct application if you already hold a first degree.

But apply earlier than 15 December if you can. Too many people apply during the four weeks leading up to the 15 December deadline. Those who apply earlier may find that their applications receive more detailed consideration, simply because the volume being handled by busy admissions tutors is less. Sometimes, too, entry standards have to be tightened, and applicants more rigorously selected as time passes. *All applications submitted by 15 December are considered*, but if you are on a two-year sixth-form or college course, give yourself a deadline of half-term, at the end of October, to submit your form to your referee.

Decisions will come from your chosen universities and/or colleges in random order. They should start to arrive a few weeks after you apply and are transmitted to you by UCAS. If you have a long wait, it probably means you are regarded as borderline. Some admissions tutors delay making decisions on those who have applied to Oxford or Cambridge University until the outcome of those applications is known.

 UCAS will acknowledge your application and will ask you to check that it has interpreted your application correctly on its computer file. Your acknowledgement will include your UCAS *application number*. Keep a careful note of this number, and if you contact UCAS or universities or colleges be prepared to quote it – it will almost certainly save time and trouble.

Decisions

Universities and colleges have to decide by 27 April whether or not to offer you a place. Before they do decide, they may call you for interview; alternatively they may offer you a place and invite you for an open day. Be prepared to travel to universities or colleges during the winter: a Young Person's Railcard or a National Express Coachcard may be a good investment.

Each decision must be one of these three:

- U: unconditional offer.
  You are in! No further qualifications are required.
- C: conditional offer.
  Still some work to do! But if you accept the offer and achieve the conditions in the examinations you are about to take, a place will be guaranteed.
- R: reject.
  Sorry – no place for you.

Replies

You have to reply to any offers you receive, but not until you have all your decisions. You will receive a Statement of Decisions from UCAS with an accompanying leaflet which tells you what to do next. The Statement will include a reply slip on which to inform UCAS which offer you wish to accept.

Statement of decisions

A statement of decisions from the (maximum of six) institutions on your form might come out as follows: (The following examples relate to applicants who are studying for A-levels.)

Conditional: BBC
Reject
Conditional: BCC
Conditional: CCC or 18 points
Reject
Conditional: 22 points

16

A-LEVEL POINTS SCORES

Note that while your A-level results will be expressed in terms of grades (eg A, B, C, D or E), offers from universities or colleges may be made in terms of grades *or* points, each grade having a points value as shown in the box:

A-Level	AS-Level
A = 10 points	A = 5 points
B = 8 points	B = 4 points
C = 6 points	C = 3 points
D = 4 points	D = 2 points
E = 2 points	E = 1 point

Note: These points values have recently been changed but the new points system will not be introduced until the year leading to entry in 2002. The new points system will also include GNVQs (renamed Vocational A-levels) and Scottish Highers and Advanced Highers.

If you are made an offer on a points basis you can usually add together whatever grades you have achieved to make up your points total. However, an overall points total in your offer may contain a requirement to obtain a specific number of points (or grade) in a particular subject. Some institutions will require the points to be achieved in your best three A-levels (or AS-level equivalent). Those Scottish students taking the Advanced Higher may find it included in their offer.

Bear in mind the precise requirements of the offer. Suppose the BCC offer requires a B in a subject you are not very confident about, whereas an offer requiring higher grades overall does not specify the B in that subject, or perhaps lets you count General Studies, then your Firm/Insurance decision (see page 18) needs to take these issues into account.

If you already have a pass or passes at A-level, make certain whether the requirements asked for relate only to the examinations which you are about to take or include the grades which you have already achieved.

In the above example you have been given four offers and you must now reduce your options to two:

- One your FIRM acceptance: you go there if you get the grades or are accepted on grades a little lower.
- One your INSURANCE acceptance: your fall-back in case your grades don't make it for your firm acceptance.

You may find that some universities and colleges with both degrees and HND courses in the same subject will send you a joint offer for both courses but with different conditions, usually lower for the HND, so that you have an automatic insurance offer should you fail to achieve the results required for the degree. These joint or double offers count as only one and you can hold *both* a firm degree/HND acceptance *and* an insurance if you wish.

TIP

IF THERE IS ANY DISCREPANCY BETWEEN THE STATEMENT OF DECISIONS AND YOUR OWN RECORD, YOU SHOULD WRITE TO UCAS IMMEDIATELY.

The statement will list your initial applications and the corresponding decisions made by each institution.

The codes used on the statement are:

U = Unconditional offer
C = Conditional offer

18

WIN £3,000!

PLUS 100 RUNNERS-UP PRIZES:
Copies of *Students' Money Matters* worth £9.99

WIN YOUR RENT!
Competition

Competition Entry Form

How To Enter

1. Please <u>underline</u> your answers clearly (a, b or c) for each of the three competition questions below.
2. Complete your name and address details overleaf.
3. Complete the questionnaire overleaf.

1 What is the maximum annual amount UK students attending a university in England or Wales will be asked to pay in tuition fees for the 2000/2001 academic year?

 a. £500 b. £750 c. £1,050

2 How much is the average student (not living at home or London-based) expected to live-on during 2000/2001?

 a. £3,725 b. £4,545 c. £5,545

3 What is the threshold annual salary graduates must be earning before they have to start paying back their student loans?

 a. £8,000 b. £10,000 c. £12,000

Trotmanpublishing

QUESTIONNAIRE

Name ....
Address ....
....
....
....
Postcode................................
Telephone ....
Sex ....
Date of Birth ....
Nationality ....
E-mail address ....

What year are you in? ....

What subjects are you taking?
Subjects   Level Predicted Grades
....
....
....
....

When will you be sitting your
exams? ....

In which year would you like to
start university? ....

Do you have internet access?
at home .... at school ......

In which regions would you
consider studying at Higher
Education?

London   yes/no
South East England   yes/no
South West England   yes/no

Midlands   yes/no
Yorkshire   yes/no
North East England   yes/no
North West England   yes/no
Scotland   yes/no
Wales   yes/no
Europe   yes/no
Outside Europe   yes/no

Which subjects are you considering
studying at Higher Education?
....
....
....

From which of the following
information sources have you
sought advice on entering Higher
Education?

UCAS Big Guide   yes/no
Degree Course Offers   yes/no
UCAS Handbook   yes/no
Student Book   yes/no
University/college   yes/no
   literature and
   prospectuses
The Complete Guides   yes/no
Other   yes/no
Internet   yes/no
   If so which site? ....

photocopy this form and
give to your friends

SEND COMPLETED FORMS TO:
'WIN YOUR RENT' COMPETITION,
2 THE GREEN, RICHMOND,
SURREY TW9 1PL.

Data Protection: Your name and address will be held on
a database and may be used to send you details of other selected
products. If you do not wish to receive this information,
please tick this box. ⬜

Conditions of entry

1. Entry Forms with three correct answers will be entered into the Prize Draw. The Draw will be made on 1st September each year, and the winner and runners-up will be notified shortly after that date.

2. Prizes: The winner will receive a cheque for £3,000. 100 runners-up will receive copies of the 6th edition of *Students' Money Matters* (RRP £9.99; published May 2000).

3. All competition entrants must be students applying for 2000 entry to university or college, or current students who will still be studying for an undergraduate or postgraduate degree in 2000.

4. Only one entry is allowed per person.

5. No purchase necessary. Separate Entry Forms are available by sending an SAE to the address given above.

Win £3,000 in our Win Your Rent Competition. You can also find this entry form at www.trotman

R = Rejection
H = Joint offer

YOUR POSSIBLE REPLIES

Firm Acceptance (F)

If you firmly accept an offer (either as UF or CF) this means that you are sure that the offer is your first preference of all the offers you have received through UCAS. You can make this reply *once only*. You will not be able subsequently to change or cancel your reply.

Insurance Acceptance (I)

If you have firmly accepted a conditional offer (CF), you may also hold one additional offer (either Conditional or Unconditional) as an Insurance acceptance (CI or UI). Obviously you would normally choose as your Insurance acceptance an unconditional offer or one with conditions that are easier for you to meet than those of your Firm acceptance.

$\boxed{\textbf{TIP}}$ Do not include as an Insurance acceptance a course which you would be unwilling to take up. If you are not accepted for your firm choice and the Insurance offer is confirmed, you are committed to go there. It would be better not to hold an Insurance acceptance than one you would not be willing to take up.

Decline (D)

If you decline an offer, you are indicating that you definitely do not wish to accept it.

Your combination of replies will be one of the following:

19

(a) Accept one offer firmly and decline any others	UF or CF D
(b) Accept one offer firmly and one as an insurance and decline any others	CF CI or UI D
(c) Decline all offers	D

Completing the reply slip

You will need to reply to each offer received with either Firm acceptance, Insurance acceptance or Decline, as summarised in the following table:

Decisions	Possible Replies	
Unconditional offer U	Firm acceptance F	(No other acceptance can be made)
	Insurance acceptance I	(Only if you firmly accept a conditional offer)
	Decline D	
Conditional offer C	Firm acceptance F	
	Insurance acceptance I	
	Decline D	
Rejection R	No reply required	

To declare your Firm acceptance of an offer write 'F' in the appropriate box alongside it on the Reply Slip. To declare an Insurance acceptance, if you

20

wish to do so, write 'I' in the appropriate box. You must then decline any other offers you have received by writing 'D' in the remaining box(es). If you firmly accept an unconditional offer of a place, you are not entitled to choose an Insurance unless you withdraw completely from UCAS.

You must complete all the blank boxes on the Reply Slip. If you leave any boxes blank UCAS will assume that you wish to decline these offers and you will lose them. For example, if you have indicated your Firm acceptance but have not selected an Insurance, UCAS will decline all your other offers and you will lose the opportunity to hold an Insurance acceptance.

If one or more of your offers is a joint offer for a degree and HND, your reply will relate to the whole joint offer. You can choose to accept the joint offer as a Firm or as an Insurance acceptance. Alternatively the joint offer can be declined. You do not have the option at this stage to accept one part of the joint offer and to decline the other.

TIP Consider your replies very carefully. Ask for advice from your school, college or careers officer. Do not accept an offer (Firm or Insurance) unless you are sure that you will be happy to enrol on the course. These commitments are binding: *you are not permitted to alter your choices at a later stage.* (There is a commitment on the institution's part as well, to accept you if you fulfil the conditions.)

TIP If you are applying for entry to courses in Art and/or Design you must carefully read the instructions published by UCAS (see also page 22) since different application and reply procedures and dates may apply depending on your choice of courses.

Once you have sent your replies to your offers, UCAS will send you a letter to confirm all the decisions made and your replies.

The flowcharts on pages 28–29 may help you understand the options open to you.

APPLICATIONS FOR MEDICAL/ DENTISTRY OR VETERINARY SCIENCE COURSES

If you wish to apply for a course leading to a professional qualification in Medicine, Dentistry or Veterinary Science (these are detailed in the *UCAS Directory*) you are allowed a maximum of four choices. Should you list more than four choices UCAS will ask you to clarify your position and reduce your choices. The closing date for applications to Medicine, Dentistry and Veterinary Science is 15 October, not 15 December as for other subjects.

APPLICATIONS FOR ART AND DESIGN COURSES

Universities and colleges can recruit to Art and Design courses via one or both of two equal pathways: Route A (Simultaneous) and Route B (Sequential).

Route A (Simultaneous)

In Route A, application forms should be submitted from September 2000 and the normal UCAS deadline (15 December) and procedures will apply. Copy application forms will be sent simultaneously to all Route A institutions listed on the form. Decisions on these applications will be due by 27 April 2001 and you will be advised in your final decision letter of the date by which you must reply to offers.

Route B (Sequential)

In Route B, application forms should be submitted from January 2001 until 24 March 2001. You are advised to get your Route B application in by 9 March 2001. If you apply through Route B you will be asked to express an interview preference (see below) and copy application forms will be sent to universities/colleges sequentially in your stated order of preference.

The timetable for Route A and Route B follows on pages 26–27.

UCAS Directory

The *UCAS Directory* will identify those courses to be recruited through Route A and Route B respectively.

Number of choices

As with all applicants through UCAS, applicants for art and design courses have up to six choices. However, because of time constraints imposed by the sequential interview (Route B) procedure, applicants choosing courses recruiting through this procedure will be restricted to a maximum of three. Such applicants may still use their remaining choices for any courses recruited through the Route A procedure. You can mix and match your Route A and Route B applications as you wish. The only constraint is that there is a maximum of three Route B choices. Your Route A choices may contain Art and Design choices or any other subject choices. For example you can apply for three Route A Art and Design choices and three Art and Design choices through Route B, or perhaps two History and two Art and Design choices through Route A and two Art and Design choices through Route B.

Application form

The normal UCAS application form is used but, in addition, a separate interview preference form will be issued for those applicants applying through Route B.

Applicants applying through both routes

If you wish to apply for courses through both Route A and B you should submit your Route A choices by 15 December. You will be able to indicate, by ticking a box on the form, that you will later wish to add choices for consideration through Route B. This will only be possible if you have not already used all six choices through Route A. At the appropriate time, UCAS will send you the necessary documentation to add choices and declare an interview preference. The facility to provide an updated personal statement and reference, if desired, will also be provided.

Decisions

Route A
(Simultaneous)
only applicants

If you only apply through Route A you will receive decisions on your choices up to 27 April. When you have received all of your decisions you will be able to accept any offers received according to the normal UCAS rules, ie you will be able to hold one conditional offer firmly (CF) plus one offer (conditional or unconditional) as an insurance (CI or UI). If you have received unconditional offers you may only hold one firmly (UF).

You will be advised in your final decision letter of the date by which you must reply to offers.

Route B
(Sequential) only
applicants

If you only apply through Route B you will receive decisions according to the timetable on page 27. If you are made an offer by your first choice and you accept it, your application will not be sent to subsequent choices. If your first choice does not make an offer your application will be forwarded to your second choice and so on.

Only one offer may be held in Route B, ie either an unconditional offer firmly accepted (UF) or a conditional offer firmly accepted (CF).

You will be required to reply to offers within seven working days or the offer will lapse. The reply date will be advised in the offer letter.

Applicants
applying through
Route A
(Simultaneous)
and *Route B*
(Sequential)

If you apply through Route A and subsequently add choices under Route B you will receive decisions as follows:

Route A: Decisions will be received up to 27 April as described above. However, there will be no facility to reply to offers through

24

Route A until your application has been considered through Route B.

If you have received offers through Route A which you wish to accept you may cancel the Route B application in order to reply to those offers.

Route B: On receipt of an offer from a Route B choice, you will receive a letter which will set out all options open to you. You will be expected to reply within seven days.

You may hold two offers (CF plus CI or UI) across Routes A and B but only *one* offer from the Route B choices.

Combination of offers held

Combination offers that can be held:

Route A		Route B
UF		None
None		UF
CF + CI		None
CF + UI		None
CF	+	CI
CF	+	UI
CI	+	CF
UI	+	CF

Notes:
(a) Only *one* offer may be held in Route B.
(b) Two offers (CF plus CI or UI) may be held in Route A according to normal UCAS rules.
(c) Two offers (any combination) may be held across Routes A and B.
(d) Only one UF offer may be held according to normal UCAS rules.
(e) It is possible to hold a CF in one Route without an insurance in either.

Confirmation   Conditional offers will be confirmed as soon as you have obtained the required qualification.

Clearing   Clearing for both Routes will operate as in the current UCAS Clearing. Clearing Entry Forms will be issued to eligible applicants during August. The Clearing Entry Form is used as a 'passport' to Clearing. Applicants approach institutions direct and UCAS is informed of acceptance. UCAS will publish vacancy information on behalf of universities/colleges.

Applicants eligible for Clearing are:

(a) those not holding any offers after consideration of initial applications;
(b) those applying too late for consideration in the normal way;
(c) those not holding a place after Confirmation decisions have been made.

Portfolio inspection schemes   UCAS hopes to publish the timetables of portfolio inspection schemes operating both within and outside UCAS.

Timetable for applications to Art and Design courses through Route A (Simultaneous)

1 September 2000	UCAS starts receiving application forms for entry in the autumn 2001.
15 December 2000	Last date for receipt of application forms.
27 April 2001	Last date for decisions on applications received by 15 December.
Up to the end of May 2001	Applicants are required to reply to offers once all decisions have been received. The 'reply by' date depends on the date by which the last decision was received. Reply dates are printed on the final decision letters.
July 2001	Clearing starts.

Timetable for applications to Art and Design courses through *Route B*

January/ February 2001	Application forms issued (to FE colleges only offering art and design courses).
24 March 2001	Last date for the receipt of forms in UCAS to be distributed to higher education institutions by 1 April. Forms received after this date will be stamped 'Late' and will receive a lower priority.
6 April 2001	First round of interviews commences. Universities/colleges start to send decisions to UCAS.
11 May 2001	Last date for decisions from first round universities/colleges. UCAS will reject by default any decisions outstanding.
17 May 2001	Second round of interviews commences and universities/colleges start to send decisions to UCAS.
8 June 2001	Last date for decisions from second round universities/colleges. UCAS will reject by default any decisions still outstanding.
12 June 2001	Third round interviews commence. Universities/colleges start to send decisions to UCAS.
10 July 2001	Last date for decisions from third universities/colleges. UCAS will reject by default any still outstanding.
July 2001	Clearing starts.

Applicants will be given seven working days in which to reply to offers. If replies are not received by the due date the offer will lapse.

The following flowcharts illustrate the Art and/or Design applications process through Route B (Sequential) and through **both** Route A (Simultaneous) and Route B.

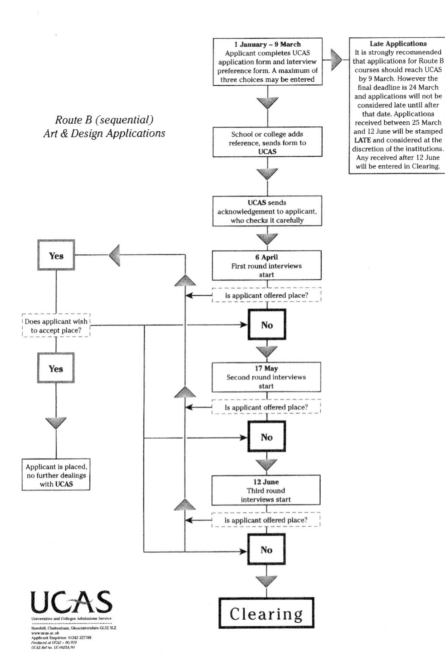

Route B (sequential)
Art & Design Applications

1 January – 9 March
Applicant completes UCAS application form and interview preference form. A maximum of three choices may be entered

Late Applications
It is strongly recommended that applications for Route B courses should reach UCAS by 9 March. However the final deadline is 24 March and applications will not be considered late until after that date. Applications received between 25 March and 12 June will be stamped **LATE** and considered at the discretion of the institutions. Any received after 12 June will be entered in Clearing.

School or college adds reference, sends form to **UCAS**

UCAS sends acknowledgement to applicant, who checks it carefully

Yes

6 April
First round interviews start

Is applicant offered place?

No

Does applicant wish to accept place?

Yes

17 May
Second round interviews start

Is applicant offered place?

No

Applicant is placed, no further dealings with **UCAS**

12 June
Third round interviews start

Is applicant offered place?

No

Clearing

UCAS
Universities and Colleges Admissions Service
Rosehill, Cheltenham, Gloucestershire GL52 3LZ
www.ucas.ac.uk
Applicant Enquiries: 01242 227788
Produced at UCAS – 00/019
UCAS Ref no. UC-0025A/01

28

Applications for Admission to Courses in Art & Design

Applications through **both** *Route A and Route B*

A maximum of six choices of institution/course is available

Route A (simultaneous)   *Route B (sequential)*

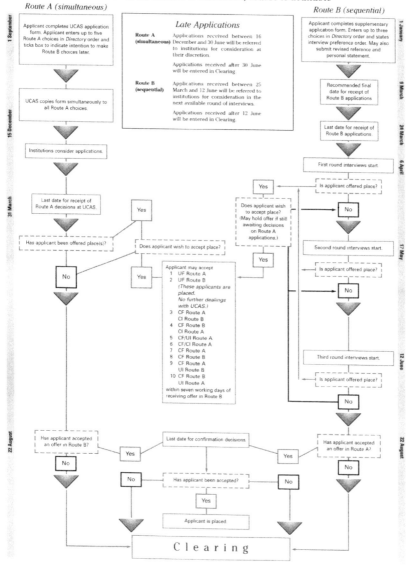

The flowchart illustrating applications through Route A only appears on page xiv

29

LATE APPLICATIONS

Avoid applying late if you can. Many popular courses fill up, and getting a place will be more difficult if not impossible. Deliberately applying late is not advised.

But if, sometime after 15 December, you decide you would like to apply, you still can. Up to 30 June UCAS will send your form to your named institutions but they will only consider you at their discretion: otherwise the same procedures are followed as for a normal application, and you will reply to offers in the usual way.

Applications received between 1 July and 20 September will be processed through the Clearing scheme which operates in July, August and September.

EXAMS AND RESULTS

Most applicants will be accepted conditionally so the results of exams taken or assessments completed in May/June are very important.

If you are ill or have some other problem that you think may adversely affect your results, tell the institutions whose offers you are holding, or ask your school or college to contact them on your behalf. Admissions tutors will do their best to take adverse circumstances into account, but must know about them before the results come out. If you leave it until after you have disappointing results, it may be too late.

TIP

After you have taken your exams it is time to relax but it is worth giving some thought to what you might do if you miss the grades required for your place – a sort of 'Plan B'. A book entitled *Clearing the Way* (published by Trotman) gives good tips on how to plan for and pick your way through Confirmation and Clearing.

Your A or AS-level results will be issued in the third week of August (Scottish Highers about a week earlier). You *must* arrange your holidays so that you are at home when the results are published. Even if all goes well and your grades are acceptable, you need to confirm your place and deal with your registration, accommodation and loan. If not, you need to take advice, find out about vacancies, and reach some quick decisions about possible offers of places in the Clearing system.

When your results are known, and have been received by the institutions, admissions tutors will compare your results with the conditions set by them.

If you have satisfied the conditions, your place will be confirmed. A university or college cannot reject you if you have met the conditions of your offer. An admissions tutor may also decide to confirm an offer even if you fail to meet some of the conditions. It is sometimes known for applicants to be accepted on much lower grades if there are places available and if there is good school or college support and perhaps a good interview record, although this varies greatly from course to course.

Before the end of August UCAS will send you an official notification of the result of your application. If your place is confirmed you will be asked to send you reply to the institution within seven days (the latest date for receipt of the reply is printed on the letter).

Applicants who have been offered a place on an alternative course to their original choice will have a choice of actions, which will be listed on the notification letter.

UCAS will supply examination results direct to the institutions for the majority of applicants taking the following examinations or courses:
GCE A-levels or AS-levels
BTEC
SQA H or A-levels
Irish School Leaving Certificate
Hong Kong A-levels
International Baccalaureate
Advanced GNVQ
You should supply your results in these examinations to the institutions only if asked to do so, except that you can avoid possible delays if you send your BTEC results to the institutions as soon as you receive them.

If you are taking any other courses such as:
SCE standard grade
GCSE
or overseas qualifications, you must send your results to the institutions where you are holding offers as soon as you receive them.

It may happen that you need to consider a change of course at this late stage. As soon as you can, look at prospectuses and reference books, and decide whether the alternative course is what you want. Since your UCAS form will again be the source document for decisions on you, it retains its importance right through to the end of the procedure. Most institutions keep it and use it as the basis of your student record file.

Retaking your A-levels
You should remember that disappointing A-levels need not mean the end of your ambitions. If low grades have prevented your being accepted on the course of your choice you may wish to consider retaking your A-levels. In some subjects and on

some syllabuses this is possible in November or January following your June exams. Alternatively, you may need to spend a full year retaking and, in that case, you may wish to consider changing to an A-level subject where you feel that you have greater aptitude and a better chance of achieving high grades.

SOME IMPORTANT POINTS

Arrange visits

Visit any university or college you are seriously interested in attending. An interview or open day may give you the opportunity: if there isn't one, write and ask to visit. It is essential to experience the place where you will spend most of the next three or four years.

UCAS publishes as part of the *Centigrade* programme (see page 6) a booklet detailing future open days and 'pre-taster' courses which it distributes to schools, colleges and careers offices in January each year.

Assess your exam prospects

Have a realistic idea of your prospects in your exams. Some admissions tutors like to give an applicant a chance even if they doubt whether he or she will make it. If you think you might not get suitable grades for entry to higher education, have alternatives ready, and applications made in good time.

Prepare for interviews

Mock interviews in school can be useful. Think about the questions that might be asked in a real interview:
• Why this subject?
• Why this department or faculty?
• Why this university or college?

and questions about
• Your A/AS-level, Higher, Advanced Higher GNVQ, or BTEC work

33

- Issues related to your chosen subject (eg genetic research, legal or political problems in the news, educational issues)
- Matters you mention in your personal statement
- Your Record of Achievement.

Anything may arise, it's true, but do your best to appear thoughtful and committed; and always have one or two prepared questions of your own about the course, opportunities after you graduate, or a relevant academic topic. Try not to ask questions only on topics covered in material already published and sent to you by the university or college.

Interviews can take different forms, for example person to person or in a group. You might be asked to take a written test. There is more advice in *Getting into Law, Getting into Mathematics, Getting into Dentistry, Getting into Medical School, Getting into Teaching, Getting into Veterinary Science* and *Degree Course Offers.*

Degree titles   Usually the first degree you get is a *Bachelor's* degree, eg:

Bachelor of Arts	BA
Bachelor of Science	BSc
Bachelor of Laws	LLB
Bachelor of Music	BMus
Bachelor of Commerce	BCom
Bachelor of Engineering	BEng

and many others.

Oxford and Cambridge Universities award a BA regardless of the subject, and allow you to upgrade it to an MA, without further exams, about four years later. Elsewhere the degree title usually, but not always, reflects the nature of the subject.

In some Scottish universities the first degree is a Master's (MA) degree. It takes four years. Most students enter university or college in Scotland at 18 after six years of secondary education; a significant minority, however, enter after only five years.

Increasingly in England and Wales Masters' degrees are being awarded for extended or enhanced courses, notably in Engineering and Science (eg MEng, MPhys, MSci).

Don't worry about degree titles. When the time comes to find a job or a place for further study, it will be the degree *content*, your personal qualities, and the standard of the work you have done, which will be important.

Honours degrees are classified as:
   First class
   Second class – upper division (2:1)
                      lower division (2:2)
   Third class

Ordinary and pass degrees are awarded, depending on the system, to those not pursuing Honours courses, or to narrow fails on Honours courses.

Sandwich courses

The general principle of a sandwich course is that it tries to integrate academic with industrial, commercial or professional training. For this reason it tends to help you in the job market; it may also entail a sponsorship which will provide you with additional money while you are a student.

• A 'thick' sandwich course (2+1+1) involves two years on the course, a year's work and a further year on the course. You may also be required to

35

work for the employer during the vacations. A 'thick' sandwich for an HND course has a 1+1+1 pattern.
- A 'thin' or integrated sandwich course alternates shorter periods of work with academic and professional study.

In many sandwich courses the institution arranges your training and you apply in the normal way through UCAS. If a sponsor requires you to go to a particular institution, that sponsor will tell you and the university or college will sort out the UCAS arrangements.

Practical information

If you are accepted, make sure you get from the university or college the information you will need about:

- Accommodation
- Term dates
- Fees
- Introductory arrangements

Some institutions send you this material as soon as you accept firmly; some only if you ask for it; some later in the procedure (even after your results). *Check in good time.*

WHAT HAPPENS TO YOUR FORM?

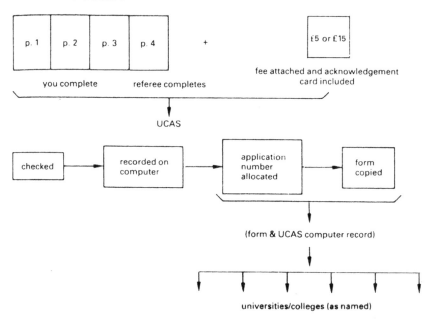

It is in the universities and colleges that the decisions are taken, usually by the academic staff who will teach you. (Note that there are different procedures if you apply for an Art and Design course through Route B (Sequential).)

WHAT ARE ADMISSIONS TUTORS LOOKING FOR?

In a few words, good students in sufficient numbers to fill their places.

Academic departments or faculties usually have admission quotas or targets – the number of students they want. Many prospectuses give an indication of the size of the intake (but remember that the numbers may include students on both single and combined or modular degrees). The bigger the intake target, usually the better your

37

chances. Students from outside the European Union do not count against quotas.

In deciding which applicants to accept, selectors are likely to be looking for:

- *Intellectual ability*
  Can you cope with the academic and professional demands of the subject and course?
- *Motivation*
  Are you aware, purposeful and realistic about yourself, and have you thought out your reasons for applying?
- *Competitive applicants*
  How well do you compare with the other applicants for the course?
- *Applicants who are likely to accept*
  If a place is offered to you, is there a good chance that you will accept it?
- *People who will make a contribution*
  Will you get involved in the life of the university or college and contribute in classes and tutorials?
- *Applicants who are likely to get the grades*
  Are you in line for the kind of exam grades this course generally commands?

WHAT DO GRADE REQUIREMENTS MEAN?

In some subjects, the department or faculty will decide that all its students need a particular qualification (say, B or C in A-level maths) in order to cope with the course.

More commonly, however, grade or points requirements are a way of rationing places. If there is high demand for a course, the 'price' in terms of exam grades will rise. High grades are an indication of *popularity*, not quality. If a department asks for three Bs, it is obvious that fewer applicants will qualify for entry than if it asks for three Cs, even though the three-C candidates might cope perfectly well with the course.

Some universities and colleges are more popular than others and can therefore set high grades if they feel that the 'market' in a particular subject will bear them. Oxford and Cambridge Universities can ask for particularly high levels of performance because schools generally encourage only those students to apply who are likely to achieve high A-level grades.

Popular courses at present include: Veterinary Science, Medicine, Law, Business Studies, Pharmacy, Sports Science, Media and Communication Studies, Psychology, Accountancy, History and English; any course with special features, such as sponsorship or an exchange with an institution overseas, may attract large numbers of applications and therefore require high grades.

WHAT IF I DON'T GET ANY OFFERS?

Talk to your school, college or careers officer. Then, if they encourage you to keep trying, approach institutions direct. In less popular subjects, there is still a chance. But it is often best to wait until you have your exam results, then contact institutions. Information about vacancies still available is published in late August at the start of the Clearing scheme. Clearing is intended to help those without a place, either because they received no offers in the first place or because their offers were not confirmed after publication of their exam results, to find one of the places remaining to be filled.

Arrangements for the publication of vacancies and the offering of 'help-line' services vary from year to year and precise sources of guidance for the summer of 2001 will be published by UCAS in the spring of that year. In 2000 for example, lists of vacancies are to be published in *The Independent*, *The Independent on Sunday* and *The Mirror* newspapers and in the electronic media of the

TIP

UCAS website (http://www.ucas.com) and CEEFAX. Official 'help-lines' are available through programmes on BBC Radios 1, 5 and Scotland and BBC2 Television. **You should ignore any other vacancy information which, in any way, claims to be 'official'.** Only UCAS publishes official vacancy information. Read *Clearing the Way* (published by Trotman) which gives good advice on how to approach Clearing and will guide you through the procedures. It also gives tips on what you might do if you do not get a place in Clearing. The following diagram is one example.

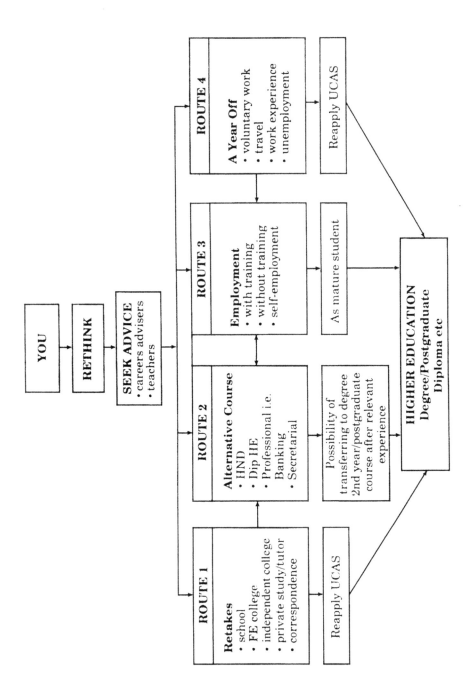

YOU

RETHINK

SEEK ADVICE
• careers advisers
• teachers

ROUTE 1

Retakes
• school
• FE college
• independent college
• private study/tutor
• correspondence

Reapply UCAS

ROUTE 2

Alternative Course
• HND
• Dip IIE
• Professional i.e. Banking
• Secretarial

Possibility of transferring to degree 2nd year/postgraduate course after relevant experience

ROUTE 3

Employment
• with training
• without training
• self-employment

As mature student

ROUTE 4

A Year Off
• voluntary work
• travel
• work experience
• unemployment

Reapply UCAS

HIGHER EDUCATION
Degree/Postgraduate
Diploma etc

41

How to Complete the Form

This chapter assumes that you will be completing the normal UCAS paper application form. Increasingly, more applicants are submitting their form electronically and although the same principles on presentation of information will refer also to these, some of the electronic processes will differ from the paper ones.

REMINDERS
- Make a photocopy of the form and practise filling it in before doing the final version on the real form.
- Write very clearly. UCAS uses image character recognition software to capture your personal data to start the computer file on your application. This saves huge amounts of time and speeds up your application. If you do not write clearly the equipment will not easily recognise what you say about yourself and it may be necessary to key in your data manually, thus losing time.
- Don't attach any loose papers to your form.
- Don't try to make more than one application in the same year.
- Once your form reaches UCAS you cannot usually amend it or add anything to it.
- Be honest and truthful.
- Read the *UCAS Directory*, and *How To Apply* which accompanies the application form. The application form consists of a series of short questions which are quite impossible to answer unless you have by your side guidance on how to complete the form contained in *How To Apply*.

DEFERRED ENTRY
If you want to apply at this stage for *deferred entry* in 2002, you should indicate this in section 3 by

putting a tick in the box headed 'Defer entry' against all those courses for which you wish to defer entry.

On page 3 of the form, section 10 enables you to explain why you want deferred entry.

Your entry might be:

---

10 PERSONAL STATEMENT (do **NOT** attach additional pages or stick on additional sheets)

Name of applicant DAVID   MORGAN

I HAVE APPLIED FOR DEFERRED ENTRY I ORDER TO GAIN WORK EXPERIENCE AND THEN VISIT NEW ZEALAND.

Bear in mind that an entry like this might provoke interview questions such as: What kind of work experience? For how long? How (whether) relevant to your chosen course? Why New Zealand? What will you do while you are there?

Here, as elsewhere, be as specific as the space allows. This kind of entry is not recommended:

---

10 PERSONAL STATEMENT (do **NOT** attach additional pages or stick on additional sheets)

Name of applicant DAVID   MORGAN

IN MY GAP YEAR I HOPE TO WORK AND TRAVEL

TIP This would cause many admissions tutors to wonder whether you had really good reasons for deferring entry, or whether you were just postponing the moment of decision about taking up a place on their course. Generally speaking, applications for deferred entry are dealt with in the normal way, but admissions tutors in some professional, science and medical subjects may be cautious – be sure you really want to defer before using this option. *If in doubt, apply for the normal year and ask the university or college*

43

where you are accepted whether it will let you defer – ie say nothing on your form about deferred entry until your plans are really firm.

It is generally a good idea to apply a year in advance, and get the formalities out of the way while you are still at school or college and available for interview. But it is also possible to delay applying to UCAS until after you have your results, and this may be appropriate in some instances.

In any event, if you wish to apply for deferred entry it is wise to check with the departments you are thinking of applying to if they are happy to admit you a year later. Some may not be and you would be wasting a choice if you applied for deferred entry there.

It is no use applying for 2002 entry in 2000–2001 if some of your exams will be taken in 2001–2002. Even though your admission is deferred, a final decision on this application has to be taken by August 2000. Furthermore you are not allowed to keep a deferred place at a university or college and then apply the following year to other institutions of the same kind. UCAS has computer programs to intercept such applications!

Do remember that if you apply for entry in 2002 and find that after all you have no useful way of spending the interim year, the institution is not obliged to take you a year earlier in 2001.

Don't be put off by all this if you are interested in deferred entry. It is, for many students, an excellent and unique opportunity to broaden their experience, and many students who would benefit a lot do not even consider the possibility.

WHO ARE YOU? Whatever you give as your title, name and address will form the basis of your UCAS and university or college record. This is fine:

1 TITLE/NAME/ADDRESS	Title M S
Surname/ Family name	R A Y
First/given name(s)	R A C H E L
Postal Address line 1	1 9 N O R T H R O A D
Address line 2	G A R S T A N G
Address line 3	P R E S T O N
Address line 4	L A N C S
Postcode (UK only)	P R 2 4 9 D E

This, however, will cause problems (and a lot of people do it):

NO

1 TITLE/NAME/ADDRESS	Title M R
Surname/ Family name	R O B A R T S
First/given name(s)	M A R K R O B A R T S

Sorry, Mark – for ever afterwards, you will be Mr MR Robarts to UCAS and the institutions.

If your name is not easily divided into 'surname' and 'first names' decide how you want to be addressed, and stick to it. For example:

1 TITLE/NAME/ADDRESS	Title
Surname/ Family name	N I K A K A M A L H A S S A N
First/given name(s)	

Chinese students, whose own custom is
to put the family name first, will normally have
to accept being addressed in the western style –
thus

1 TITLE/NAME/ADDRESS	Title		
Surname/ Family name	W O N G		
First/given name(s)	C H U – H A I A N G E L A		

will appear as C H A WONG. It is just possible that
institutions may address you as Wong Chu-hai, but
don't count on it! If you have adopted a western
name, feel free to include it.

The address section should not present any
problems provided that you write boldly and
clearly. Be careful about the difference between 3, 8
and B. Abbreviate your county in the normal way –
see 'LANCS' in the example above.

The correspondence address is the one that
will appear in the UCAS record, and that is
where correspondence about your application
will be sent. You are at liberty to have your letters
sent anywhere you choose – for example, your
school.

Once you leave school in June, you will need to tell
UCAS to send correspondence to your home
address – it will not do it automatically. (Tell your
universities and colleges as well.) If you do not
inform UCAS, offers of places at Confirmation or
details of Clearing opportunities will be sent to your
school. There will then be a delay in your receiving
them and you could lose a place as a result.

46

Postal Address line 1	F	O	R	S	Y	T	H		H	O	U	S	E	
Address line 2	T	H	E		Q	U	E	E	N	'	S		S	C	H	O	O	L
Address line 3	K	E	N	D	A	L								
Address line 4	C	U	M	B	R	I	A							
Postcode (UK only)	L	A	2	5		6	W	X						

Main contact number (including STD/ area code)	Tel:	0 1 5 3 9 5 7 9 8 6 4
	Fax:	

Home address (if different)	'GATEWAYS'
	ROCKINGHAM ROAD
	HATTON, WARWICK
Postcode (UK only)	C V 3 8 2 E A

It is very important that you include your postcode. Include your fax number and email address if you have one, or if you or perhaps your parents have access to one. Fax and email messages can speed up communication dramatically at Confirmation and Clearing time.

NO

UCAS presorts its letters for the Post Office by using the postcode, and correspondence with you might be delayed if you do not put it on your form. Equally you must write the postcode clearly. In the following example the correct postcode is RH and the address is in West Sussex but, perhaps understandably, the operators read the code as RM and letters to the applicant were delivered to Upminster in Essex:

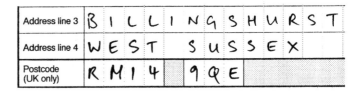

Address line 3	B I L L I N G S H U R S T
Address line 4	W E S T S U S S E X
Postcode (UK only)	R M 1 4 9 Q E

Some admissions tutors like to communicate with their applicants by telephone, so do state your telephone number if you have one.

MORE PERSONAL DETAILS

2 FURTHER DETAILS

Your age on 30 September 2001:

Years   Months

Male (M)/ Female (F)

Student Registration Number for vocational qualifications or Scottish Candidate Number (SCN)

Date of birth

Disability/special needs (including dyslexia)/medical condition

Fee code   Student Support Arrangements

Date of first entry to live in the UK

Area of permanent residence _____

Residential category

Country of birth _____

Nationality _____

48

This looks more complicated than it actually is. Write in the boxes.

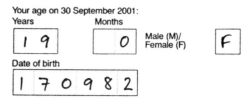

Your date of birth is required for UCAS and institutions' records, and must be correctly written. Some people who fill in the form in 2000 will write:

NO

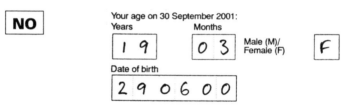

Elementary – but a lot of people do it! At the last count 8% of all applicants were apparently born in the year in which they applied!

Others have difficulty with arithmetic:

NO

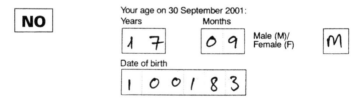

No – it is not your age now, but at the date of your entry into higher education that is required. This applies even if you are applying for deferred entry in 2002: give your age on 30 September 2001.

Disability/ Special needs

Disability/special needs (including dyslexia)/medical condition

49

The question on disability/special needs is intended to give a short indication of your possible need for any special arrangements. It is also intended to provide statistics on the numbers applying for and being admitted to higher education. Information in the *How To Apply* booklet makes it clear how you should code yourself. You will be asked to indicate whether you are *registered* disabled. If you consider yourself to be in need of special help you should state your needs in section 8 (see page 82). In your own interests give relevant information here: you will *not* be rejected because of the answer you give, whatever it is.

SQA/SCOTVEC

Student Registration Number for vocational qualifications or Scottish Candidate Number (SCN)

If you have completed or are completing a qualification awarded by SQA or SCOTVEC, enter the appropriate registration number in the box provided. Ask your college if you do not know your number. This information could be very important if there is any delay in getting your results to a university or college where you are holding an offer. It could mean the difference between landing a place or losing it!

Student support arrangements

Student Support Arrangements   Fee code

Since 1998, new entrants to full-time higher education in the United Kingdom have been expected to make a contribution towards the tuition fee costs of their course. This amount is dependent upon family income. Around a third of students pay the full amount, around a third pay nothing and the remainder pay an amount somewhere in between. The maximum payable in the 2000–2001 year is £1050. Assessment of the actual amount of tuition fees payable will be carried out by your

Local Education Authority (LEA) if you live in England and Wales. In Northern Ireland, assessment will be carried out by your Northern Ireland Education and Library Board.

Recent decisions made by the Scottish Parliament mean that no tuition fees will be paid up front by those resident in Scotland wherever they study in the UK. However, all those who graduate will have to pay an 'HE endowment' when their salary reaches a certain level.

All England, Wales and Northern Ireland domiciled applicants are advised to apply for assessment in order to establish their eligibility for assistance in future years, even if they expect to have to pay the full amount in their first year. Applicants from England and Wales should write the name of their LEA, eg Essex. Those from Northern Ireland should write the name of their Board, eg North Eastern Area.

If you are a European Union applicant you may be eligible to have all or part of your tuition fees paid. You should apply to the appropriate authority for the institution at which you firmly accept an offer, as follows:

- For institutions in England and Wales you should apply to the DfEE (the institution at which you have firmly accepted an offer will be able to provide you with further details of whom to contact).
- For institutions in Scotland or Northern Ireland you should contact SAAS (Student Awards Agency for Scotland) or the Northern Ireland Education and Library Board respectively.

You are advised to apply to the appropriate authority as soon as you have firmly accepted an offer of a place. You should not wait until a conditional offer is confirmed later in the year.

You should enter one code from the table below, in the box provided, to show who is expected to pay your tuition fees.

The effect of the new arrangement means that the majority of UK and European Union applicants will find themselves in category 02 of the table below, and you should enter 02 if you are *eligible for assessment* for an LEA (or SAAS or Northern Ireland Education and Library Board) award, even if you expect that your parents' income or spouse's income will be too high for you actually to receive assistance.

List of fee payers and codes

01 Entire cost of tuition fees paid by private finance

02 Applying for assessment of eligibility for tuition fee contribution to Local Education Authority (LEA), Student Awards Agency for Scotland (SAAS) or Northern Ireland Education and Library Board

03 Contribution from the Department for Education and Employment

04 Contribution from a Research Council

05 Contribution from the Department of Health or a Regional Health Authority

06 Overseas student award from UK Government or the British Council

07 Contribution from a Training Agency

08 Other UK Government award

09 Contribution from an overseas agency (eg overseas government, university, industry)

10 Contribution from UK industry or commerce

90 Other source of finance

99 Not known

In cases where applicants have an arrangement for all or part of their tuition fee contribution or costs to be paid by an award from any other agency or body (eg industry/commerce or a training agency) a relevant code should be selected from the remaining values.

Only applicants who will be funding the entire cost of their tuition fees by their own private finance, and who are *not eligible* for an LEA (or SAAS or Northern Ireland Education and Library Board) award should enter code 01.

At the time of application, you may not be clear whether or not sponsorship will actually be awarded to you, and you may be applying to a number of companies at the same time. In these circumstances indicate the name of your first choice sponsor. If the outcome of the application for sponsorship affects your year of entry, apply initially for 2001 entry, but indicate in section 10 that you might wish to defer subsequently to 2002 entry.

Date of first entry to the UK and residential category

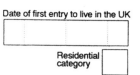

Date of first entry to live in the UK

Residential category

If you were born outside the UK you should enter the date when you first entered the UK to live. Do not put down the date when you first arrived for a holiday or a short study visit for example.

Residential category can be more complicated and it is important because what you write here will be the point from which institutions will start to classify you as 'home' or 'overseas' for the purpose of tuition fees. Those classified as 'overseas' pay a *much* higher level of fee, which will usually be at least £6000, and for some courses up to £16,000, by 2001. Your tuition fee status has no direct connection with your nationality. It depends on your place of ordinary residence and the length of time you have been ordinarily resident there.

Full details of how to complete the residential category box are given in the UCAS *How To Apply* booklet. You should read it very carefully.

Because of the complexity of the residential category regulations the following step-by-step process has been devised by UCAS in association with the United Kingdom Council on Overseas Students Affairs. Words or phrases underlined are explained in the footnotes to the questionnaire.

Category Summaries:

A UK/EU national, Channel Islands/Isle of Man resident or child of UK/EU national, who has lived for three years in the EEA – but not solely for full-time education.

B Settled in the UK for three years, but not solely for full-time education.

C Refugee, or person granted Exceptional Leave to Enter/Remain, living in UK since status recognised/granted, or such person's husband, wife or child.

D National of Iceland, Liechtenstein or Norway, living in the UK and employed as a migrant worker, or such person's husband, wife or child, living in EEA but not solely for full-time education.

G UK/EU national, or child of UK/EU national, normally living in EEA but temporarily employed outside EEA.

O Other.

---

1. Are you, or either of your parents, citizens of the UK or of another European Union country[1]?
   a) Yes   Go to question 2
   b) No[2]   Go to question 5

2. By 1 September 2001, will you have been living in the UK or elsewhere in the European Economic Area[3] (EEA) for the previous three or more years, apart from temporary absences?
   a) Yes   Go to question 3
   b) No   Go to question 4

3. Do you normally live outside the EEA[3], but currently live in the EEA[3] **only** to attend full-time education?
   a) Yes   Your residential category code is O
   b) No   Your residential category code is A

4. Have you been living outside the EEA[3] because you, or a partner, husband or wife have been temporarily employed elsewhere?
   a) Yes   Your residential category code is G
   b) No   Your residential category code is O

5. Are you, your husband or wife or a parent recognised by the UK Government as refugees[4], or have you or they been granted Exceptional Leave to Remain[4] in the UK following an asylum application?
   a) Yes   Go to question 6
   b) No   Go to question 7

6. By 1 September 2001, will the person with this status have been living in the UK continuously (apart from temporary absences or temporary employment abroad) since refugee status was recognised or since Exceptional Leave[4] was granted?
   a) Yes   Your residential category code is C
   b) No   Your residential category code is O

7. By 1 September 2001, will you have been living in the UK for at least three years, apart from temporary absences or temporary employment abroad?
   a) Yes   Go to question 8
   b) No   Go to question 10

8. Do you normally live outside the UK, but you currently live in the UK **only** to attend full-time education?
   a) Yes   Your residential category code is O
   b) No   Go to question 9

9. Is the length of your stay in the UK currently limited by immigration control[5]?
   a) Yes   Your residential category code is O
   b) No   Your residential category code is B

10. Are you, your husband or wife or either of your parents a national of Iceland, Liechtenstein or Norway?
   a) Yes   Go to question 11
   b) No   Your residential category code is O
11. Did you, your husband or wife or one of your parents move to the UK for employment, and has that person been employed since last entering the UK apart from brief absences?
   a) Yes   Go to question 12
   b) No   Your residential category code is O
12. By 1 September 2001, will you have been living in the EEA^3 for the previous three years, apart from temporary absences or temporary employment abroad?
   a) Yes   Go to question 13
   b) No   Your residential category code is O
13. Do you normally live outside the EEA^3, but you currently live in the EEA^3 **only** to attend full-time education?
   a) Yes   Your residential category code is O
   b) No   Go to question 14
14. If you entered the UK because of your husband's or wife's employment here, are you still in the UK with him or her?
   a) Yes/not applicable   Your residential category code is D
   b) No   Your residential category code is O

Notes:

[1] The European Union includes the following countries: Austria, Belgium, Denmark (excluding the Faroe Islands and Greenland), Finland, France (including the French Overseas Departments of Guadeloupe, Martinique, French Guyana, Reunion, Saint-Pierre et Miquelon), Germany (including Heligoland), Greece, the Republic of Ireland, Italy, Luxembourg, the Netherlands, Portugal (including the Azores and Madeira but excluding Macao), Spain (including Ceuta, Melilla, the Balearic Islands and the Canaries), Sweden, the United Kingdom (with Gibraltar).

If your answer to question 1 is 'no' and your category code is 'O', but you or either of your parents are subsequently granted EU citizenship, you should immediately inform your chosen universities and colleges.

3 The European Economic Area includes the countries of the EU plus Iceland, Liechtenstein and Norway.

4 The Home Office will have sent you a letter confirming your status if you are officially recognised as a refugee or if you have been granted Exceptional Leave to Enter or Remain.

5 Anyone whose stay in the UK is limited by immigration control will have their passport or travel document endorsed. If your answer to question 9 is 'yes' and your category code is 'O' but you are granted British citizenship or Indefinite Leave to Remain on or before 1 September 2001, your chosen universities or colleges may reconsider your residential category. You should inform them immediately if this happens.

If you find this section difficult to complete as (for example) you live overseas because of your parents' work, classify yourself as best you can, and be prepared for questions from the institutions. They will try to be fair to you, but they do have a duty to apply the regulations justly to all their students. You could, before applying, write to institutions outlining your circumstances. Some overseas companies have standard letters for employees to use. It sometimes happens that universities and colleges will classify the same student in different ways, depending on their reading of the rules.

Area of permanent residence

Area of permanent residence __CLEVELAND__

Country of birth __ENGLAND__

Nationality __BRITISH__

In the *How To Apply* booklet it makes it clear what you are to write against the *Area of permanent residence* part of the form. If you live:

- *outside the UK,* name the country (eg Australia)
- *in Scotland,* name the District or Islands Area (eg Clackmannan)
- *in Greater London,* name the London borough (eg Bexley)
- *in a former Metropolitan District,* name the district (eg Sefton)
- *elsewhere in the UK,* name the county (eg Leicestershire)

This information is used for statistical purposes only, to find out where applicants come from. It will not be used for selection purposes.

Country of birth
Nationality

Country of Birth and Nationality should be straightforward matters of fact. Your nationality is what appears in your passport.

YOUR LIST OF APPLICATIONS

3 APPLICATIONS IN *UCAS DIRECTORY* ORDER					If you wish to apply later for Art & Design Route B courses please tick (✓)			
(a) Institution code name	(b) Institution code	(c) Course code	(d) Campus code	(e) Short form of the course title	(f) Further details requested in the *UCAS Directory*	(g) Point of entry	(h) Home	(j) Defer entry

It is often best to complete section 3 last of all, having dealt with all the factual information required of you, and having also worked out your entry in section 10.

This is one of the crucial parts of the form. Let's start with the mechanics of it.

Your choices

3	APPLICATIONS IN *UCAS DIRECTORY* ORDER	
	(a) Institution code name	(b) Institution code
	A S T O N	A 8 0
	B U W E	B 8 0
	C O V N	C 8 5
	P O R T	P 8 0
	S H E F D	S 1 8
	W A R W K	N 2 0

Note:

- Universities and colleges must be listed in the order in which they appear in the *UCAS Directory*.
- Universities and colleges are referred to by their *abbreviated names*. Some applicants try to write out the full name, out of either respect or pedantry. Use the university/college code name.
- You are allowed a maximum of *six* applications (you can apply to fewer than six if you wish, but are not allowed to add applications later unless you wish to apply to a course or courses in Art and Design through *Route B* (see page 22) or you apply to only one course (see page 1). In this latter case you will be allowed to add an extra application or applications but only if you pay the difference between the single and the multiple application fee (£5 or £15 respectively).
- Use a separate line for each entry; no gaps; no

59

crossings out; clear and correct numbers (UCAS sorts copy forms by code numbers, not university/college names).

- Universities and colleges are not listed in preference order unless you apply for courses in Art and Design in *Route B* when you will be asked to indicate your interview preference order.

Courses

3 APPLICATIONS IN *UCAS DIRECTORY* ORDER				
(a) Institution code name	(b) Institution code	(c) Course code	(d) Campus code	(e) Short form of the course title
E H C	E 4 2	N I 2 6		BA / BMS
H U D D S	H 6 0	N I 2 0		BA / BS
L E E D S	L 2 3	N I 0 0		BA / Mgt St
N O R T H	N 7 7	N I 2 0	C	BA / Bus S
P O R T	P 8 0	N I 2 0		BA / Bus St
S T R A T	S 7 8	N I 5 0		BA / Bus

Note:

- Although these are similar courses, they do not all have exactly the same code – you need to check the code for *each course* carefully.
- Some courses are taught at franchised institutions, ie away from the main university or college. This is indicated in column 3 (d), eg the Carlisle campus of the University of Northumbria in the above example.
- A surprising number of people (8% of all applicants) apply for courses which don't exist eg by putting down a course code for one institution when that course is taught at a

different institution! Have the *UCAS Directory* at your elbow when filling in the form.

TIP

- This is a *consistent* choice of courses. An admissions tutor will have a clear idea of this student's aims, and will be favourably impressed by his or her *motivation* for Business and Management Studies.

This emphasis on consistency of course choice should not prevent you from choosing the courses you really want. But be prepared to defend a selection of courses that lack a common thread; and try to cover yourself in your personal statement (see page 84).

NO

Reminder: check required entry grades in *University and College Entrance* and *Degree Course Offers*, and try not to apply to six popular institutions which all demand high grades. This is difficult to illustrate because the situation varies from subject to subject, and a good applicant may have little to fear. But beware, for example, of applying for English at six universities such as:

Bristol	Nottingham
Edinburgh	Oxford
University College London	York

TIP

Entry to all these universities and colleges in English is very competitive, and even with high predicted A-level grades you cannot be sure of acceptance. Better to name at least one university or college which is not so popular, and preferably one that makes offers at a slightly lower level – the reference books will help.

This advice applies in many subjects, but *all* Medical schools and most Law schools are highly competitive and you should apply to those whose courses appeal to you.

If there is one particular university or college you want to attend (perhaps because you are a mature student and can't move away from home) then you can use your choices to apply for more than one course, like this:

3	APPLICATIONS IN *UCAS DIRECTORY* ORDER					If you wish to apply later for Art & Design Route B courses please tick (✓)			
(a) Institution code name	(b) Institution code	(c) Course code	(d) Campus code	(e) Short form of the course title	(f) Further details requested in the *UCAS Directory*	(g) Point of entry	(h) Home	(i) Defer entry
S U N D	S 8 4	G 5 2 3		BA/BC				
S U N D	S 8 4	H 6 1 1		MEng/CSE				
S U N D	S 8 4	G 5 0 0		BSc Comp				
S U N D	S 8 4	H 6 2 0		MEng/ComE				

Knowing how competitive entry is to courses in humanities and social science, you may name courses in related subjects.

At some universities or colleges it is not necessary to apply for more than one course because admission is to a faculty or group of related subjects. This is usually explained in the *UCAS Directory*.

Don't apply for courses you are not really interested in, simply in order to fill up the form.

Art and Design courses

As has been noted on page 22 there are two routes for application for courses in Art and Design. If you wish to apply for courses in *Route A* (Simultaneous) you do so by indicating your choices in section 3. If you wish later also to apply through *Route B* (Sequential) you should indicate your intention by putting a tick in the box. UCAS will send you additional documentation later to enable you to make your *Route B* choices. In this case you can list up to five choices in section 3.

The *UCAS Directory* indicates which courses recruit through *Route A* (Simultaneous) and which through

3 APPLICATIONS IN *UCAS DIRECTORY* ORDER					If you wish to apply later for Art & Design Route B courses please tick (✓)				
(a) Institution code name	(b) Institution code	(c) Course code	(d) Campus code	(e) Short form of the course title	(f) Further details requested in the *UCAS Directory*	(g) Point of entry	(h) Home	(j) Defer entry

Route B (Sequential). Note that many courses will consider applicants through both routes. Route B is intended primarily for those students following an Art Foundation Course but Foundation Course students have in the past successfully gained places on courses through UCAS procedures with a 15 December closing date.

Before deciding whether to apply through Route A and/or Route B you should take advice from your school, college, course tutor or careers officer. The UCAS/Trotman publication, Art & Design Courses 2001, which details all Art and Design courses recruiting through UCAS, indicates the proportions of students to be admitted through Route A and Route B to each individual course.

Examples of applications through Route A are:

3 APPLICATIONS IN *UCAS DIRECTORY* ORDER					If you wish to apply later for Art & Design Route B courses please tick (✓) ✓				
(a) Institution code name	(b) Institution code	(c) Course code	(d) Campus code	(e) Short form of the course title	(f) Further details requested in the *UCAS Directory*	(g) Point of entry	(h) Home	(j) Defer entry
B MTH	B 5 0	W 2 7 0		BA/Anim					
H ERE	H 1 8	W 2 1 5		BA/Ill					

This example is for an applicant who is trying for Art and Design places through Route A but intends to make further applications through Route B later in the applications cycle.

The following example is for an applicant who wants to apply for a course in Art and Design through *Route A* as well as non-Art and Design courses but also wishes later to apply for further courses in *Route B*.

3 APPLICATIONS IN *UCAS DIRECTORY* ORDER						If you wish to apply later for Art & Design Route B courses please tick (✓)	✓		
(a) Institution code name	(b) Institution code	(c) Course code	(d) Campus code	(e) Short form of the course title	(f) Further details requested in the *UCAS Directory*		(g) Point of entry	(h) Home	(i) Defer entry
C O V N	C 8 5	H 7 7 0		MDes/IPD	MDes FT				H
C U W I C	C 2 0	W 2 3 0		BA/ID					
L B R O	L 7 9	H 7 7 5		Mix/IDTec					

Remember that you can freely mix and match your courses both in Art and Design and other subjects. The only constraint is that you have a maximum of three choices in *Route B* all of which must be Art and Design courses as indicated in the *UCAS Directory*.

HNDs
Many universities and colleges offer BTEC or SQA Higher National Diploma (HND) courses in addition to degrees, and in many institutions the HNDs are an integral part of a departmental or faculty academic structure. Put simply, this means that you will usually find that there will be both degree and HND courses in the same subject area with the opportunity for students to transfer between them. You will need to bear this in mind

TIP
when planning your applications strategy. First, remember that with few exceptions HNDs fall into two main subject areas, Science and Engineering, or Business Studies and related subjects. Your approach to these areas should be quite different.

Science and Engineering courses at all levels attract relatively fewer applications than Business and Finance and so it is quite likely that if you apply for a degree in, say, Mechanical Engineering at an institution which also offers an HND in

64

Engineering, admissions tutors will use UCAS procedures to make you an offer which will cover both the degree *and* the HND but with different conditions for each – normally lower for the HND.

If you feel that you will reach the minimum entry standards required for a degree course, you should aim for this in subject areas such as Science and Engineering, unless you positively want to take an HND, which many students do.

For HND courses in Business Studies and related subjects the picture is rather different. They usually attract a large number of applications in their own right as many students opt for the shorter and often more specialised nature of the courses: and it is very unusual for institutions to make dual offers for degrees and HNDs. This means that you must consider your options very carefully. If you have any doubt about your ability to reach the level required for degree entry, usually a minimum of 16–20 points in A or AS-levels or a BTEC National Award with 3 or 4 distinctions and the remaining units at merit in final year units, you will probably be best advised to apply for the HND. Many institutions offer common first years for degree and HND students, allowing transfers to take place at the end of year one directly into the second year of the degree course for those who reach an acceptable level in the first year of the HND. There is even a chance, though a slim one, that if your A-level or BTEC results are much better than expected the institutions offering you the HND may instead give you the chance of a late degree place.

Clearly, you *must* consult your school, college or careers office before making these difficult decisions.

Of course, there are some very special subjects where the number of courses available is limited and you may only have the option of the HND – for example Management of Textile Aftercare, Minerals Resource Management or Leather Technology.

University/ college diplomas

Some universities and colleges offer undergraduate diplomas (defined as a full-time or sandwich two- or three-year diploma which attracts a mandatory student maintenance award). Your policy with regard to application should be the same as for HNDs.

Previous applications

If you have applied before, don't try to hide the fact. Indeed, it may help if the universities and colleges can identify your previous application, especially if they made you an offer you failed to achieve. They can look up their interview records or their previous notes on your application, and may decide to give you another chance.

All you do is complete this section of the form:

If you have previously applied to any institution(s) listed above enter the institution code(s) and your most recent UCAS application number (if known)

If you cannot remember your previous UCAS number, just give the year.

While most university and college departments consider retake candidates, and some welcome the greater maturity and commitment to hard work that those retaking demonstrate, some will demand higher grades. It is always worth checking with the relevant admissions tutor that your proposed retake programme is acceptable. It is very rare for

Oxford or Cambridge to accept applicants who have retaken their exams.

'Further details requested'
On many UCAS forms section 3(f) is completely blank. But further information is often requested, and you must follow the instructions in the *UCAS Directory*. The sort of entry you need to make may be:

- 3-year or 4-year course
- choice of Oxford college (maximum of three)
- minor, subsidiary or first-year course option choice
- specialisations within chosen degree (eg Biology).

Point of entry
If you think you may be qualified for credit transfer or 'entry with advanced standing' (entry at second-year level or perhaps third-year level in Scotland) you should check this possibility with the institutions to which you wish to apply. Use section 3(g) to indicate this to the universities or colleges by putting 2 or 3 (ie the year of proposed entry) against *each* application to which this is relevant.

The home column
If you are willing to live at home while attending a particular university or college, enter H in the Home column on the right-hand side – an example is given in the multiple application on page 64. This information is unlikely to make a difference to your chances of acceptance but may help institutions plan their accommodation requirements.

Defer entry
If you wish to defer entry to any of the courses you list until 2002, tick the appropriate box. You will need to explain in section 10 why you want to defer entry and what you intend to do in your 'year out'.

PREVIOUS EDUCATION

4 SECONDARY EDUCATION/FE/HE	From Month	From Year	To Month	To Year	PT, FT or SW	UCAS SCHOOL OR COLLEGE CODE
JOHN HIRAM HIGH SCHOOL, LONDON W18	09	94	06	99		
ST CUTHBERT'S SIXTH FORM COLLEGE,	09	99				
LONDON W20						

Most applicants have little difficulty here – this is a common sort of entry. There is no need to mention your primary school! If you spent some time at a school overseas, include it. If you have been at several schools (as can happen, for example, if a parent is in the armed services) list those where you spent most time, and *always include your present school or college.*

If you have spent any time at a higher education institution you must mention it, and be prepared for questions about what happened.

Mature students should complete this section as fully as possible (many forget to list their present college). A mature student's entry might look like this:

4 SECONDARY EDUCATION/FE/HE	From Month	From Year	To Month	To Year	PT, FT or SW	UCAS SCHOOL OR COLLEGE CODE
COURCY HIGH SCHOOL	09	77	07	81	FT	
SILVER BRIDGE COLLEGE	09	99	07	00		
BARCHESTER COLLEGE OF TECHNOLOGY	09	00				

RECORD OF ACHIEVEMENT/ PROGRESS FILE

5 Tick (✔) if you have a National Record of Achievement or Progress File (UK applicants only)	pre-16		post-16	

If you have an up-to-date (post-16) National Record of Achievement (NRA) or Progress File, indicate that here. Do not attach your NRA/Progress File documentation to the form. You should take your full Record of Achievement or Progress File with you if invited for interview as part of the selection process. If you wish, send a brief summary (*not* the full record) to the institution, quoting your application number. You should be prepared to discuss and explain what the Record/File comprises, and how it was developed.

If you have an NRA for your education up to age 16, but not an up-to-date one, indicate this within section 10.

OCCUPATIONAL BACKGROUND

6	ADDITIONAL INFORMATION (not used for selection purposes)
A	Occupational Background SYSTEMS ANALYST
C	UCAS may send you information from other organisations about products and services directly relevant to higher education applicants. Please tick the box if you *do not* want to receive it. ☐

The instructions attached to the form included in *How To Apply* ask you to give the occupation of the parent or other person who brings the highest income into the home in which you have been brought up. Universities and colleges, and also government and researchers, need to know about the demand for higher education from within the various socio-economic groups and how well that demand is being satisfied. For example, now that the new student loans system mean that students have to fund their study from their own money, it is important to know whether this is having an effect on demand and take-up of higher education among less well-off families.

The information that you supply in this section will *not* be passed by UCAS to admissions tutors in

universities and colleges until after all decisions on
your application have been made.

ETHNIC ORIGIN

B   Ethnic Origin
(UK applicants only) [ ][ ]

The instructions on how to complete the form
included in *How To Apply* tell you to state the
category which broadly corresponds with the
origin of your recent forebears: read them carefully,
then give the information as requested.

Some important points about this section:

- *Do not worry about it.* (Whatever you write will
  not be seen by the universities or colleges, and
  will *not* affect the decision on your application.
  When your form is copied the whole of section 6
  is omitted, and the individual computer record
  will not be available to institutions.)
- If your permanent home is outside the UK, leave
  it blank.
- Otherwise do complete it. (As with the
  information you supply on occupational
  background – see above – your ethnic origin will
  not be passed by UCAS to admissions tutors
  until after all decisions on your application have
  been made. Only then will it be possible for
  institutions, when they get statistics after the end
  of the admission process, to be sure that they are
  treating fairly applicants from different origins.)

EXAMINATIONS – TAKEN AND TO BE TAKEN

We can take sections 7A and 7B together – the same
principles apply to both.

GCE, GCSE, SQA

For many applicants the entry will be straightforward but it still requires care. Examples:

7A QUALIFICATIONS COMPLETED (Examinations or assessments (including key/core skills) for which results are known, including those failed)

Examination/Assessment centre number(s) and name(s)

ALLINGTON COMPREHENSIVE SCHOOL, CENTRE NO. 7164001

Examination(s)/Award(s)					Examination(s)/Award(s)				
Month	Year	Awarding body	Subject/unit/module/ component	Level/ qual	Result Grade Mark or Band	Month	Year	Awarding body	Subject/unit/module/ component	Level/ qual	Result Grade Mark or Band
06	99	AQA	ENGLISH LANGUAGE	GCSE	B					
			MATHEMATICS		B					
			GEOGRAPHY		A					
			FRENCH		C					
			CHEMISTRY		D					
			PHYSICS		B					
			ART		A					
			COMPUTER STUDIES		B					

7B QUALIFICATIONS NOT YET COMPLETED (Examinations or assessments (including key/core skills) to be completed, or results not yet published)

Examination/Assessment centre number(s), name(s) and address(es)

ALLINGTON COMPREHENSIVE SCHOOL, CENTRE NO. 7164001

Examination(s)/Award(s)					Examination(s)/Award(s)				
Month	Year	Awarding body	Subject/unit/module/ component	Level/ qual	Result	Month	Year	Awarding body	Subject/unit/module/ component	Level/ qual	Result
06	01	AQA	ECONOMICS	A						
		AQA	GEOGRAPHY	A						
		AQA	MATHEMATICS	AS						
		AQA	DESIGN	AS						

Note:

- If a place or a date clearly relates to several exams, there is no need to repeat it.
- Use the abbreviations shown on the form and in the *How To Apply* booklet on how to complete the form. If in doubt, ask your school or college for information about (for example) exam centre numbers.
- Include everything, even if not 'passed'. You must not conceal fails. You sign at the bottom of page 3 to say you have, to the best of your knowledge, given complete and accurate information throughout your form:

12 **DECLARATION:** I confirm that the information given on this form is true, complete and accurate and no information requested or other material information has been omitted. I have read *How to Apply*. I undertake to be bound by the terms set out in it and I give my consent to the processing of my data by UCAS and educational institutions. I accept that, if I do not fully comply with these requirements, UCAS shall have the right to cancel my application and I shall have no claim against UCAS or any higher education institution or college in relation thereto. Applicant's Signature.. Date	**tick one** I have attached payment to the value of £15.00/£5.00 or I have attached a completed credit/debit card payment coupon

- Be careful to distinguish between
  AS – Advanced Supplementary (half A-levels)
  SP – Special Papers, taken in addition to A-levels
  STEP – Cambridge Sixth Term Entry Papers (of little or no relevance to your applications to institutions other than Cambridge University).
- List your exams in date order. There is no required order for exams which were taken at the same sitting.
- If you have completed or are studying for modular A or AS-level examinations you should state in the 'subject/unit/module/component' column the title of the overall qualification. You need not list individual modules or give module results.

What will they look for? This part of your form is bound to be examined carefully by admissions tutors. At GCSE or the equivalent they will be looking for:

- a reasonable spread of background qualifications
- signs of quality
- fulfilment of the course entry requirements
- a sound basis for sixth-form (or equivalent) work
- key subjects: English language and maths. Even if the university or college does not require them, most employers do.

Many admissions tutors attach a lot of importance to your results at GCSE. After all they will usually be the only evidence of your academic achievement to date.

In considering your entry in section 7B (Qualifications not yet completed), they are looking for:

- the right subjects to satisfy entry requirements
- subjects they are prepared to include in an offer
- how many A-level and AS-level subjects you are taking, or what qualifications you are offering instead
- gaps in your record that you are trying to fill: for example by taking GCSE alongside your A and AS-levels.

TIP

As we have already seen, three A-levels or the equivalent (eg two A-levels plus two AS-levels), the Advanced GNVQ or five Scottish Highers, are the norm for a degree place; some applicants are offered places even though they are taking only two A-levels, but not, as a rule, in competitive subject areas. It is worth checking whether you might be considered on fewer subjects, by looking in prospectuses or contacting institutions. Note that the colleges of higher education are more likely than the universities to accept two A-levels or the equivalent. Of course the usual requirement for admission to an HND course is one A-level but very popular courses, eg in Business Studies, may ask for two.

 TIP

Some institutions publish lists of subjects they recognise for admission purposes, and if you are taking, for example, two subjects from among Art, Design and Technology, Home Economics and Communication Studies, this is well worth checking.

A-level General Studies is accepted by some departments, but not others. (It is more likely to be considered in the newer universities and in the colleges of higher or further education.)

Admissions tutors will also be on the watch for students who are repeating A-levels. Give full details of your results at the first attempt, say what you are repeating and when, and try to apply realistically.

Additional exams

You can include any other exams you wish, for example:

• Associated Board exams in Music: state instrument, most recent grade (you need not mention all of them), dates, and mark
• Guildhall and LAMDA exams
• RSA and Pitman exams (if you think they are relevant)
• Youth Award Scheme

and so on.

Ask yourself: is this exam in any way relevant to my application?

74

Another example, showing repeat exams as well:

7A QUALIFICATIONS COMPLETED (Examinations or assessments (including key/core skills) for which results are known, including those failed)

Examination/Assessment centre number(s) and name(s)

SILVERBRIDGE COLLEGE, CENTRE NO. 647011

Examination(s)/Award(s)					Result	Examination(s)/Award(s)					Result
Month	Year	Awarding body	Subject/unit/module/ component	Level/ qual	Grade Mark or Band	Month	Year	Awarding body	Subject/unit/module/ component	Level/ qual	Grade Mark or Band
06	98	OCR	ENGLISH	GCSE	B	06	99	NEAB	GEOGRAPHY	GCSE	C
			MATHEMATICS		B						
			BIOLOGY		A	06	00	NEAB	BIOLOGY	A	C
			CHEMISTRY		B				CHEMISTRY	A	N
			FRENCH		C				ART + DESIGN	A	E
			HISTORY		D						
			GEOGRAPHY		D						
			ART		B						

7B QUALIFICATIONS NOT YET COMPLETED (Examinations or assessments (including key/core skills) to be completed, or results not yet published)

Examination/Assessment centre number(s), name(s) and address(es)

SILVERBRIDGE COLLEGE, CENTRE NO. 647011

Examination(s)/Award(s)						Examination(s)/Award(s)					
Month	Year	Awarding body	Subject/unit/module/ component	Level/ qual	Result	Month	Year	Awarding body	Subject/unit/module/ component	Level/ qual	Result
06	01	OCR	CHEMISTRY	A							
			ART + DESIGN	A							

BTEC (EDEXCEL)

Setting out BTEC qualifications is a little complicated. Section 7A should contain the details of any qualifications already completed and awarded eg the BTEC First Diploma. Section 7B is for qualifications still to be achieved. However, if you are already partway through a qualification eg BTEC National Diploma, which by definition you have still to finish but part of which you have already had assessed, you should set out those units which you have completed in section 7B.

Indicate the qualifications completed or being aimed for on the first line of sections 7A or 7B as appropriate and then list the units taken. Use the 'level' column to indicate both the level of your

7A QUALIFICATIONS COMPLETED (Examinations or assessments (including key/core skills) for which results are known, including those failed)

Examination/Assessment centre number(s) and name(s)

SILVERBRIDGE COLLEGE, BARSETSHIRE

Examination(s)/Award(s)					Result Grade Mark or Band	Examination(s)/Award(s)					Result Grade Mark or Band
Month	Year	Awarding body	Subject/unit/module/ component	Level/ qual		Month	Year	Awarding body	Subject/unit/module/ component	Level/ qual	
			FIRST DIPLOMA IN BUSINESS AND FINANCE								
06	99	LE	WORKING IN ORGANISATIONS	F(3.0)	P						
"	"	"	FINANCE	F(1.0)	D						
"	"	"	INFORMATION PROCESSING	F(1.0)	M						
"	"	"	SALES	F(1.0)	M						
"	"	"	KEYBOARDING	F(1.0)	P						
"	"	"	WORD PROCESSING	F(1.0)	M						

7B QUALIFICATIONS NOT YET COMPLETED (Examinations or assessments (including key/core skills) to be completed, or results not yet published)

Examination/Assessment centre number(s), name(s) and address(es)

SILVERBRIDGE COLLEGE, BARSETSHIRE

Examination(s)/Award(s)					Result	Examination(s)/Award(s)					Result
Month	Year	Awarding body	Subject/unit/module/ component	Level/ qual		Month	Year	Awarding body	Subject/unit/module/ component	Level/ qual	
			NATIONAL DIPLOMA IN BUSINESS AND FINANCE			06	00	LE	ORGANISATION	N(2.0)	
						"	"	"	PEOPLE IN ORGANISATIONS	N(1.0)	
06	01	LE	ORGANISATION (M)	N(2.0)		"	"	"	ACCOUNTS	N(1.0)	
"	"	"	PEOPLE IN ORGANISATIONS (M)	N(1.5)		"	"	"	MARKETING	N(2.0)	
"	"	"	FINANCE (M)	N(2.0)		"	"	"	INFORMATION PROCESSING	N(1.0)	
"	"	"	INFORMATION PROCESSING (M)	N(1.0)		"	"	"	BUSINESS LAW	N(1.5)	
"	"	"	WORD PROCESSING (M)	N(1.0)							
"	"	"	SPANISH (P)	N(1.0)							

76

units and also their value, putting the value in brackets, eg F (1. 0). Where you have completed units as part of a qualification still to be completed indicate your performance in each unit by stating your measure of success in brackets after the title of each unit, ie P (Pass) M (Merit) D (Distinction).

GNVQs   The relatively new Advanced GNVQ qualifications are difficult to set out clearly. There are a lot of subject/unit titles to include and, remembering that the form is photo-reduced when sent to universities and colleges, try to save on words or repeating yourself. The Electronic Application System, on the other hand, provides a purpose designed section for GNVQ results. Admissions tutors will be looking for the result of the whole assessment as well as what units you have completed to make up the whole qualification.

Assessment centre number and name
- The school or college GNVQ centre number should be entered into the initial section of the form, together with the centre name and address.

Awarding body
- The awarding body should be noted in the appropriate column. This is particularly helpful where it can clarify the optional units taken. Codes for entering awarding bodies are available in the UCAS form instructions in *How To Apply*.

Listing the Advanced GNVQ qualification
- If you are likely to offer complete Advanced GNVQ programmes as your main qualification you should begin completing section 7B by writing the full title of the GNVQ programme in the 'subject/unit/module/component' column. This title should be underlined, to make it clear for admissions tutors. The level will be AGNVQ for Advanced GNVQ applicants.

A full list of Advanced GNVQ units completed or to be taken prior to HE entry should then be completed. After a mandatory vocational unit the code (MAN) should be written; for optional vocational units the code (OP) is required. The mandatory core skills, Application of Number, Communication and Information Technology, should be written down fully and the level (3–5) indicated.

If you have fully completed a GNVQ unit, by completing all the performance criteria and (if appropriate) the unit test, the code 'CU' should be entered into the results column after the relevant unit. NOTE: the code 'CU' can be used before internal or external verification has occurred. It will simply give an admissions tutor some idea of how far through the GNVQ programme you are.

Part Advanced GNVQ qualifications or units of Intermediate GNVQ

- If you are completing some units of an Advanced GNVQ programme, the full title of the Advanced GNVQ programme should be indicated and underlined, then you should list the units you plan to complete using the coding system: mandatory vocational unit (MAN); optional vocational unit (OP) – you should make it clear that you only intend to cover some units by writing 'Part Qualification' after listing the units in section 7B.

Some applicants will be completing an Intermediate GNVQ alongside a GCE A-level course. Details of the Intermediate GNVQ studied should be entered fully, as described for the Advanced GNVQ except that the number of units will be fewer and the levels will be IGNVQ for Intermediate GNVQ and 2–5 for key skills.

Additional studies

- If additional GNVQ units are being studied, they must be listed, with either AGNVQ or IGNVQ to

78

indicate the level. The code (ADD) should be used after the unit to clarify it is additional to the requirements for the GNVQ programme title. Therefore, if you are taking a mandatory unit from another GNVQ title as additional studies or an additional recommended key skills unit, the code (ADD) should be used. Also, where possible, the number of additional units likely to be taken should be indicated in brackets underneath the list of additional GNVQ units. This will help the admissions tutor to interpret the qualification.

Where NVQ units are being taken, the title of the NVQ should be listed and underlined. Individual unit titles should be entered separately, with an indication of whether the total NVQ is likely to be completed prior to HE entry. Where A-levels, AS examinations, or GCSEs are studied they should be entered onto the form with the level (ie GCSE or GCE).

- The column width is very narrow for writing down unit titles. It may be necessary for you to write over lines to enter all the titles as is shown in the following example. Text should, however, be contained within the area of the page/grid defined by the bold outer black line.

If both Intermediate and Advanced have been covered together, you should only list the Advanced qualifications in full.

If the BTEC National Diploma is achieved through 'accreditation of prior learning' alongside the GNVQ course, the Advanced GNVQ programme should be listed in full. It will confuse admissions tutors if both qualifications are included.

7A QUALIFICATIONS COMPLETED (Examinations or assessments (including key/core skills) for which results are known, including those failed)

Examination/Assessment centre number(s) and name(s)   99999 SMALL TOWN SCHOOL

Month	Year	Awarding body	Subject/unit/module/component	Level/qual	Result Grade Mark or Band	Month	Year	Awarding body	Subject/unit/module/component	Level/qual	Result Grade Mark or Band
06	98	LEAG	CHEMISTRY	GCSE	E	06	99	AQA	• ORGANISING A BUSINESS VENTURE	(OP)	
"	"	MEG	ENGLISH	"	C				• APPLICATION OF NUMBER	2	
"	"	NEAB	FRENCH	"	B						
"	"	SEG	HISTORY	"	E				• COMMUNICATION	2	
"	"	ULEAC	MATHEMATICS	"	D				• INFORMATION TECHNOLOGY	3	
06	99	AQA	BUSINESS	GNVQ	M						
			• BUSINESS ORGANISATIONS AND EMPLOYMENT	(MAN)		06	99	RSM	PIANO	GRADE5	MERIT
			• PEOPLE IN BUSINESS ORGANISATIONS	(MAN)		06	99	OCR	MATHEMATICS	GCSE	C
			• CONSUMERS AND CUSTOMERS	(MAN)							
			• FINANCIAL AND ADMINISTRATIVE SUPPORT	(MAN)							
			• BUSINESS AND THE ENVIRONMENT	(OP)							

7B QUALIFICATIONS NOT YET COMPLETED (Examinations or assessments (including key/core skills) to be completed, or results not yet published)

Examination/Assessment centre number(s), name(s) and address(es)   01234 METROPOLIS COLLEGE OF FE
HIGH STREET, METROPOLIS AN1 2AR

Month	Year	Awarding body	Subject/unit/module/component	Level/qual	Result	Month	Year	Awarding body	Subject/unit/module/component	Level/qual	Result
06	01	OCR	BUSINESS	GNVQ		06	01	OCR	• INFORMATION TECHNOLOGY	4	
"	"	"	• BUSINESS IN THE ECONOMY	(MAN)	CU						
"	"	"	• BUSINESS ORGANISATIONS AND SYSTEMS	(MAN)	CU	"	"	"	• STATISTICS	(ADD)	
"	"	"	• MARKETING	(MAN)	CU	"	"	"	• BUSINESS IN THE COMMUNITY	(ADD)	
"	"	"	• HUMAN RESOURCES	(MAN)	CU				(2 ADDITIONAL UNITS)		
"	"	"	• PRODUCTION AND EMPLOYMENT IN THE ECONOMY	(MAN)							
"	"	"	• FINANCIAL TRANSACTIONS COSTING AND PRICING	(MAN)		06	01	AQA	FRENCH		A
"	"	"	• FINANCIAL FORECASTING AND MONITORING	(MAN)							
"	"	"	• BUSINESS PLANNING	(MAN)							
"	"	"	• BUSINESS LAW	(OP)	CU						
"	"	"	• BUSINESS AND THE EUROPEAN UNION	(OP)	CU						
"	"	"	• MANAGEMENT INFORMATION SYSTEMS	(OP)							
"	"	"	• MARKETING RESEARCH AND STATISTICS	(OP)							
"	"	"	• APPLICATION OF NUMBER	3							
"	"	"	• COMMUNICATION	3							

KEY/CORE SKILLS You should list details of key/core skills acquired (7A) or to be acquired (7B) for example through Modern Apprenticeship or the ASDAN Universities Award Scheme.

SCOTTISH QUALIFICATIONS If you are offering qualifications awarded by SQA or its predecessor bodies SEB and SCOTVEC you should read the instructions issued by UCAS on completing the application form very carefully. The new National Qualification framework in Scotland is difficult to lay out on paper and you will need to exercise great care here.

'Unorthodox' qualifications

Ensure that you give enough information to enable your application to be considered fully. If it will not all go on the form, summarise it on the form and send a letter with details to *each university or college* you name (not to UCAS), quoting your application number.

| TIP |

The instructions on how to complete the application form included in *How To Apply* give guidance to those applying with international or overseas qualifications. *International* and *European Baccalaureate* are widely accepted and can easily be accommodated on the form – there is enough room in section 7 to specify what you are taking and at what level. For exams of *other countries*, be as specific as possible, giving the title of the exam in your own language and listing the subjects if there is room; if not, adapt the form in the best way you can. In the American system, which is also used in other countries, a brief summary of grades and test scores can be given on the form, and any Advanced Placement papers should certainly be listed separately, but it will be essential to send your full transcript, just as you would to an American school. Don't wait to be asked for it, but send your transcripts and other materials direct to your

81

chosen institutions as soon as you know your UCAS application number.

In any overseas exam, always say what is the maximum mark available, and remember that entry to higher education in the United Kingdom is competitive and therefore you must often have above-minimum qualifications.

SPECIAL NEEDS

8 SPECIAL NEEDS or **SUPPORT** required as a consequence of any disability or medical condition stated in Section 2.	

You have already been asked to indicate in section 2 any disability or special needs, so that the information can be conveniently gathered for statistical purposes. Section 8 invites you to give details of any such physical or other disabilities or medical conditions. Some applicants are reluctant to use this section of the form, either because they don't want to draw attention to themselves or because they think their chances of acceptance will be adversely affected. This is misguided. Institutions need to know of any measures they must take to cope with your needs:

- so that they can make any necessary allowance (for example, they may be willing to lower entry requirements to allow for serious difficulties)
- so that they can be sure that they can provide the special arrangements or facilities you need.

Please do *not* leave it to your referee to mention problems, because your referee's report is normally confidential and its contents cannot be discussed with you.

82

TIP If you need to make an entry here, it is a good idea to check with the universities or colleges *before* *applying* whether they can meet your particular needs. Some campuses are better than others for wheelchairs, some have special facilities for the visually handicapped or the deaf. Fieldwork may be a problem, but there may be other ways of structuring your course.

Be prepared to visit any institution to which you are thinking of going. This is important advice for all applicants, but *particularly* for those in this category.

If you claim special consideration on account of dyslexia, be prepared to provide independent evidence (usually a psychologist's report). Admissions tutors will need to be convinced that you can keep up with the required work.

PREVIOUS EMPLOYMENT

9 DETAILS OF PAID EMPLOYMENT TO DATE Names and addresses of recent employers	Nature of work	From		To		PT/
		Month	Year	Month	Year	FT

It is often useful for admissions tutors to know if you have had a job or work experience. This can be particularly helpful if you have worked in an area relevant to your application or chosen career. Full-time and part-time jobs (including weekend ones) may be worth including, but only if they have been continued for a reasonable period. Even if the jobs you have had were just to earn you pocket money, an admissions tutor will see this as a broadening of

83

your experience. Note that institutions undertake *not* to contact previous employers for a reference without your permission.

PERSONAL STATEMENT

10 PERSONAL STATEMENT (do NOT attach additional pages or stick on additional sheets)
Name of applicant DAVID MORGAN

Section 10 is important because it is the only part of the application form where you have a chance to select and emphasise points about yourself. The instructions in *How To Apply* encourage you to say something about:

- your career aspirations
- your reasons for choosing the course
- the name of any sponsor you may have. Relatively few students are sponsored through their course and you will not be at a disadvantage if you have nothing to include in this section. Institutions are keen to know, however, if you have been able to secure this form of financial support. If you have applied for sponsorship but do not yet know whether you have been successful, say where you have applied
- relevant background or experience, which may include work experience, or work shadowing, practical activity in music or theatre, attendance at courses, time abroad (you should explain why this is relevant)
- any interests, including sports, you may have which are not strictly relevant to the course, but help to give an impression of you as a person.

(Mature students read on, but see also page 91.)

84

Some principles
- Think about the impression you want to give
- Organise the material
- Write very clearly, and don't try to pack too much in
- Only put in things you are prepared to talk about at interview
- Check the spelling!
- Don't repeat material that already appears on the application form.

NO

Each year there are a few applicants who leave this section completely blank. Obviously that is inadvisable! But many do themselves no good simply as a result of the way they present information. These are *real* examples to illustrate the pitfalls (though they have been made clearer to read than they were in the copies institutions received):

---

10 PERSONAL STATEMENT (do NOT attach additional pages or stick on additional sheets)

Name of applicant   RUTH KNIGHT
READING   KNITTING   WALKING

Is this all you have to say?

Name of applicant DAVID MORGAN

I HAVE BEEN INTERESTED IN ACCOUNTING FOR QUITE A LONG TIME AND THAT'S BEEN ONE OF THE REASONS I TOOK ACCOUNTS AT GCSE. I WAS HOPING TO DO ACCOUNTS AT A-LEVEL BUT IT WAS NOT AVAILABLE AT MY SCHOOL. I HAVE HAD SOME WORK EXPERIENCE IN ACCOUNTING DURING YEAR 10 AT SCHOOL. I FOUND A PLACEMENT AT ELECTROLUX ACCOUNTS DEPT. FOR A WEEK AND ENJOYED IT VERY MUCH. WE WERE UNABLE TO DO WORK EXPERIENCE IN YEAR 12 DUE TO INSURANCE PROBLEMS. I THINK THE CAREER PROSPECTS ARE GOOD FOR ACCOUNTING WITH MANY REWARDS.

I AM QUITE ACTIVE AND ENJOY SPORTS LIKE SQUASH, TENNIS, FOOTBALL AND GOLF. MY MAIN SPORT IS GOLF AND I AM A MEMBER OF THE LOCAL GOLF CLUB PLAYING OFF A HANDICAP OF 15. I HAVE REPRESENTED MY SCHOOL AT GOLF LAST YEAR AT SEATON CAREW AND HOPE TO PLAY AGAIN THIS YEAR.

This was an attempt to do it properly, and there are a few useful points: but the general impression is superficial and negative. The applicant has not given enough thought to the impression created on a critical reader. At least he has been specific about his sporting interests: too many people just write 'reading' or 'music'. And it is accurately spelt – such things matter.

Here now are some examples of how to use this section effectively:

86

Name of applicant CHRIS MOORE

I AM PRESENTLY SECRETARY OF THE SOCIAL COMMITTEE FOR YEARS 12 + 13 WHICH ARRANGES SOCIAL EVENTS AND ALSO ATTEMPTS TO IMPROVE FACILITIES. I HAVE ALSO HELD THE POSITION OF HOUSE CAPTAIN AND ALSO BEEN INVOLVED WITH VARIOUS SPORTS TEAMS AND SUBJECT-RELATED CLUBS.

APTER ABANDONING MY CHILDHOOD DREAM OF BECOMING AN ASTRONAUT, I BECAME DRAWN TOWARDS THE LEGAL PROFESSION. SUBSEQUENTLY MY WORK EXPERIENCE IN YEAR 11 WAS AT ONE OF SHEFFIELD'S LARGEST SOLICITORS. DURING THE TWO WEEKS I WAS THERE I SPENT A BRIEF TIME IN COMMERCIAL, MATRIMONIAL AND POLICE PROSECUTION DEPARTMENTS. ALL THESE ASPECTS OF LAW WERE INTERESTING BUT MY EXPERIENCE IN THE CRIMINAL LAW DEPARTMENT WAS VERY STIMULATING AND IS THE AREA WHICH I HOPE TO PURSUE A CAREER IN - ULTIMATELY IN THE CAPACITY OF A BARRISTER.

OUTSIDE OF SCHOOL I AM A MEMBER OF A LOCAL SUB-AQUA BRANCH HELPING IN MOST ASPECTS OF THE CLUB, ESPECIALLY THE MAINTENANCE AND ADMINISTRATION OF EQUIPMENT AND THE TRAINING (THEORETICAL AND PRACTICAL) OF OTHER MEMBERS. I AM A KEEN CYCLIST AND TENNIS PLAYER AND MY OTHER INTERESTS LIE IN MODERN CINEMA AND HOROLOGY. I ALSO ENJOY TWO PART-TIME JOBS WHERE MY DUTIES RANGE FROM GARDENING, LABOURING AND DRIVING, TO SHOPKEEPING, STOCKTAKING AND THE USE OF AN ELECTRONIC TILL.

 TIP Note the much more convincing justification for the choice of course; a selector would feel that thought had gone into this. It might have been better to put the second paragraph first. Hit the reader with your main point, and *do not* worry about filling the entire space.

The second example is tauter and says everything that needs saying:

87

Name of applicant SIMON CHESTER

I INTEND TO STUDY SCIENCE RELATED SUBJECTS AS I FIND THEM INTERESTING.
I BELIEVE THE SCIENCES ARE THE KEY TO THE FUTURE DEVELOPMENT OF THE
NATION AND I INTEND TO BE A PART OF THIS. DURING MY EARLY SCHOOL
CAREER I HELD VARIOUS POSITIONS OF RESPONSIBILITY. I WAS MY FORM'S REPRESENTATIVE
ON THE YEAR COUNCIL FOR THREE YEARS. IN THE FINAL YEAR I WAS
APPOINTED A PREFECT.
    DURING THE FIVE YEARS, I TOOK AN ACTIVE INTEREST IN SPORTS. I WAS
A MEMBER OF THE BASKETBALL TEAM, IN A SPORT IN WHICH I TOOK A
REFEREEING COURSE. I WAS ALSO THE SCHOOL DISCUS CHAMPION
    AT SIXTH FORM I HAVE BEEN ELECTED SENIOR STUDENT. THIS POST
INVOLVES MANY RESPONSIBILITIES, INCLUDING ATTENDING FUNCTIONS SUCH
AS MEETING THE PRESIDENT OF LITHUANIA. AS A STUDENT COUNCILLOR I
HAVE BEEN RESPONSIBLE FOR THE PRODUCTION OF THE 1994 YEARBOOK.
    I AM A MEMBER OF THE COLLEGE DEBATING SOCIETY. I HAVE
DEBATED TOPICS RANGING FROM ANIMAL EXPERIMENTS TO FEMALE EQUALITY.
    I AM AN ACTIVE MEMBER IN THE COLLEGE CHARITIES GROUP. WE
HAVE HELD KARAOKE SESSIONS IN THE LUNCH HOURS, AND NON-UNIFORM
DAYS; IN TOTAL WE HAVE RAISED OVER £4,000. OUTSIDE COLLEGE I
WORK IN A LOCAL SOUP KITCHEN FOR THE HOMELESS.
    I HAVE RECENTLY BEEN ELECTED TO REPRESENT THE YOUTH OF
BLACKPOOL ON THE BLACKPOOL POLICE AND COMMUNITY FORUM.

These applicants realise that they are applying for competitive courses, and set out to sell themselves, without going over the top. Always emphasise experience which is relevant to your chosen courses; be specific about details; try to sound an interesting person; in case you get an interview, give an interviewer plenty of 'leads'.

This section of the form is especially important in subjects like creative and performing arts. Say what you have done, seen or heard. Don't be one of the music applicants who do not actually mention their chosen instrument! If you have any useful practical experience it should be mentioned – something which may be vital to the success of an application to a medical or veterinary school, and may also significantly assist if you are applying for some management and engineering courses.

If you are currently studying for an Advanced GNVQ, with which admissions tutors are still relatively unfamiliar, explain the relevance of your GNVQ studies to the course(s) for which you are applying.

If you are a sports person give details of your achievements. 'I play tennis' adds little; 'I play tennis for the county' shows that you excel in something.

If you have chosen a career, mention it and say why your selected courses are relevant to it. Applicants for teacher-training education courses should be sure to give details of school experience (time and place).

To sum up Admissions tutors are usually looking for students who can analyse their current experiences and give clear reasons why these have led to an application for the courses chosen. This becomes difficult for an applicant where he or she has selected a wide range of disparate courses.

The text and presentation of the section provides the admissions tutor with an indication of your communication skills, in terms of basic spelling and grammar, and also the ability to express information and ideas clearly. Overall, the section can provide useful evidence of maturity of thought, sense of responsibility, and if you intend to study away from home, an indication of your likely ability to cope in a new environment.

There is a danger that applicants do not use this section effectively to justify their application. A common weakness is that applicants tend to describe what they are doing now rather than to analyse their current experiences and relate them to what they hope to get from degree or HND level study.

Alongside the descriptive approach tends to go a listing of data already present elsewhere on the form (ie present studies) or details of apparently unrelated hobbies. Hobbies are an important part of the personal statement, but they need to be analysed in the context of how they have contributed to the development of your generic skills or personality in a way that would support success on the higher education courses to which you have applied.

In all of this section, be *honest and specific*. If necessary, be selective – there are only 24 hours in a day, and claiming too much is unnecessary. Similarly, rambling on simply to fill up the space is likely to be counterproductive!

TIP Try working with friends while preparing your personal statement (and by definition you will be helping them as well). Read through each other's drafts – you will be surprised how often a friend will say to you 'but haven't you forgotten your. . .'.

MATURE STUDENTS

There is no single definition of a 'mature' applicant, but most of higher education now classifies students as mature if they are over 21 years of age at the date of entry to the course.

UCAS publishes a booklet specifically aimed at potential mature students entitled *The Mature Student's Guide to Higher Education*. It is available free of charge direct from UCAS.

Most departments welcome applications from mature students, and many (especially in science) would like more. As a mature student, you are more likely to be accepted with qualifications that are unorthodox or would simply not be enough if they were presented by a student aged 18 or 19 in full-time education (for example, one A-level for entry to a degree course). But do bear in mind that there is competition for places, and that in most subjects places are not kept aside for mature students. If you are favourably considered, you are likely to be called for interview.

It is not usually advisable to rely on qualifications gained several years ago at school. University and college departments will want to see recent evidence of your academic ability so that they can evaluate your application fairly. In addition, taking a course of study at the right level helps prepare you for full-time student life. In most parts of the country there are 'access' or 'foundation' courses specially designed for mature students; or you can take a BTEC/SQA, GNVQ/GSVQ course, A or AS-levels or Scottish Highers.

Before you apply, ask the universities or colleges for any special information they publish on mature student entry. Tailor your application accordingly.

The UCAS form is not ideal for many mature students although section 10 has been extended to virtually a full page in order to give you more space in which to describe your life. If you have gone back to college as a full-time student aged, say, 22, you should find no particular difficulty; in section 10 say something about your time since leaving school. But if, like many mature applicants, you are rather older and have had a variety of occupations and experience, you may find the application form restrictive. In this case you can, if you wish, summarise your career on the form and send a full curriculum vitae direct to your chosen institutions. However, section 10 is big enough to present your background and interests in fair detail. Everyone's circumstances are different, but the following example is the kind of thing that might attract an admissions tutor's favourable attention.

Name of applicant   IAN BROWN

1972   LEFT SCHOOL AGED 16, NO QUALIFICATIONS
1972 - 78   VARIOUS PERIODS OF TRAVEL, MANUAL WORK + UNEMPLOYED
1978 - 86   R.A.F. (INCLUDED TECHNICAL TRAINING)
1986 - 98   SELF - EMPLOYED (MOTOR REPAIRS)
1999 - 00   ACCESS COURSE, SILVERBRIDGE COLLEGE (FULL-TIME) WITH
             A VIEW TO ENTERING LAW SCHOOL

MOST OF MY EXPERIENCE HAS BEEN IN MANUAL TRADES, BUT I NOW
THINK I HAVE THE ABILITY TO CHANGE DIRECTION. I HAVE KNOWN
MANY PEOPLE WHO HAVE TAKEN DEGREES AND I THINK I CAN MAKE
A SUCCESS OF IT.
     MY INTEREST IN LAW WAS AWAKENED BY A FRIEND'S PROBLEM
OVER AN INSURANCE CLAIM. I TRIED TO HELP HER AND STARTED
EXPLORING THE LAW BOOKS IN THE LIBRARY. I REALISED THAT THIS WAS
AN INTELLECTUAL CHALLENGE I COULD RELATE TO. SINCE THEN I
HAVE DONE MORE READING AND VISITED THE COURTS. I HAVE
STARTED TO HELP IN THE CITIZENS' ADVICE BUREAU. NOW I WANT
TO QUALIFY AND HOPE TO WORK IN A COMMUNITY LAW CENTRE.
     MY NON-ACADEMIC INTERESTS INCLUDE TRAVEL (IN VARIOUS
COUNTRIES), MOTOR CAR RESTORATION AND SOCIALISING.

The entry in section 7B that would go with this
might be written thus:

Examination/Assessment centre number(s), name(s) and address(es)

SILVERBRIDGE COLLEGE, CENTRE NO. 647011

Examination(s)/Award(s)					
Month	Year	Awarding body	Subject/unit/module/ component	Level/ qual	Result
06	01		CORE MODULES &	ACCESS	
			OPTIONS IN		
			SOCIOLOGY		
			ECONOMIC HISTORY		

CRIMINAL
CONVICTIONS

11 CRIMINAL CONVICTIONS: Do you have any criminal convictions? See *How to Apply* YES ☐   NO ☐

If you have been convicted of a criminal offence (excluding (a) a motoring offence for which a fine and/or a maximum of three penalty points were imposed or (b) spent sentences), you are required to declare this by completing the YES box in section 11 of your form. If you have not been convicted of a criminal offence you must complete the NO box.

You should be aware that for certain courses particularly related to Teaching, Health and Social Work programmes, any criminal conviction, including spent sentences and cautions, must be declared. If you are in doubt you should contact the appropriate institution and seek advice.

Serving prisoners

If you are currently serving a prison sentence you must show the prison address for correspondence in section 1 of your application form, and in addition you must complete the YES box in section 11.

94

Rehabilitation of Offenders Act 1974

Applicants with criminal convictions should be aware of the provisions of the Rehabilitation of Offenders Act 1974 as they affect those with spent sentences. Advice about whether you will be required to declare a conviction can be obtained from a solicitor, the National Association for the Care and Resettlement of Offenders (NACRO), the Probation Service or the Citizens Advice Bureau.

If your circumstances change after you have applied (for instance, you are convicted of a criminal offence) you must declare this information to UCAS and to any institution to which you have applied or may apply during this application cycle.

Note:

(a) Applicants or their advisers who wish to declare additional material information but do not wish to do so on the UCAS form, should do so by writing direct to the admissions officers at the institutions listed on their form or at any other institution considering their application.

(b) False information will include any inaccurate or omitted examination results.

(c) Omissions of material information will include failure to complete correctly the YES/NO box in section 11 of the application form relating to criminal convictions or to declare any other information which might be significant to your ability to commence or complete a course of study. If you fail to tick the YES/NO box your application will not be passed on to universities or colleges until you do so. UCAS will ask you to indicate a specific answer to this question if you do not do so when first submitting your application form.

DECLARATION

By signing this form you are saying that the information you have provided is accurate and complete and that you agree to abide by the rules of UCAS. You are also agreeing to your personal data being processed by UCAS and institutions under the relevant data protection legislation. Any offer of a place you may receive is made on the understanding that, in accepting it, you agree to abide by the rules and regulations of the institution.

In pursuance of the prevention of fraud, UCAS reserves the right to disclose information given in your application form to outside agencies, eg Police, Home Office, Local Authorities, Examining Boards, Department of Social Security, the Student Loans Company.

If UCAS or an institution has reason to believe that you or any other person has omitted any mandatory information requested in the instructions on how to complete the application form included in *How To Apply* or on the application form, has failed to include any additional material information (see note c) (above), has made any misrepresentation or given false information, UCAS and/or the institution will take whatever steps it considers necessary to establish whether the information given in your application is correct. UCAS and the institutions reserve the right at any time to request that you, your referee or your employer provide further information relating to any part of your application form, eg proof of identification, status, academic qualifications or employment history. If such information is not provided within the time limit set by UCAS, then UCAS reserves the right to cancel your application. Fees paid to UCAS in respect of applications that are cancelled as a result of failure to provide additional information as requested, or for providing fraudulent information, are not refundable.

REFERENCES The reference that appears on page 4 of your form is in some ways the most important item in the selection process. It is only your referee who can tell the admissions tutor about your attitude and motivation, and who can comment on your ability so that admissions tutors are not reliant solely on the results you write in section 7A, and the exams to be taken which you list in section 7B.

In the *How To Apply* booklet are listed the points of particular concern to admissions tutors, including:

* academic achievement and potential
* suitability and motivation for the chosen course
* personal qualities
* career aspirations.

Referees are also asked to estimate your level of performance in forthcoming exams, and these predictions are important to your chances of acceptance.

Note that, as a result of the *Data Protection Act 1998*, you have the right to see your reference. You should contact UCAS if you want to see what your referee has written about you. You will be charged £5 to receive a copy of the reference. There is now, unlike in previous years, no such thing as a 'confidential reference'.

Work hard, and impress your referee!

Your reference will normally come from your present school or college, or the one you attended most recently. If you choose anyone else, make sure it is someone who can provide the kind of assessment higher education institutions need. But if you are attending a school or college it will look very odd if you choose someone from outside. On no account should your reference come from a relative. If you find it impossible to nominate an academic referee, find someone who can at least comment objectively on your personal qualities and motivation, and ability to cope with a degree or HND course. An application which contains no reference will be returned to you by UCAS.

Good luck!